WOLFGANG BORSICH
TRAVEL GUIDE
LANZAROTE

We recommend our road map
◄ **THE LANZAROTE MAP**
See illustration on page 2

Text:
Wolfgang Borsich
Photos:
José María Barreto Feo
Wolfgang Borsich
Walter Fogel
Barbara Graf
Peter Sickert
Pedro Velázquez
With thanks to Peter Sickert for his kind
permission to reproduce photograph no. 10
from the series Collection Peter Sickert,
Lanzarote 8/10 inch, 1988, p. 156/157
Layout:
Wolfgang Borsich
Prepared for printing:
Wolfgang Borsich
Fish water colour:
Jan Černý
Drawings and maps:
Gerd Oberländer
I.S.B.N.: 84-89023-03-4
Depósito Legal: M. 21.273-1994
Imprime: Mariar, S. A. 28045 Madrid

English edition 1994

THE MAP OF
LANZAROTE

+ **Brief guide**
In words & pictures
With **descriptions of the**
major places & sights
With **notes on Canarian food**
With **RECOMMENDED RESTAURANTS**
With **recommended accommodation**
With **vital information**
With **INSIDER** tips

EDITORIAL YAIZA S.L.

Contents

General Travel Tips

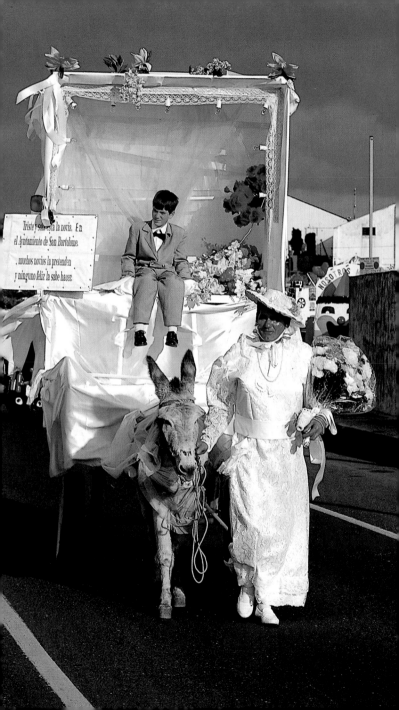

Triste y sola está la novia. En
el ayuntamiento de San Bartolomé.

... muchos novios la pretenden
y ninguno feliz la sabe hacer.

Using this Book

First Impressions is intended to put you in the mood for the island and characterise Lanzarote at the same time.

In the first big chapter **At the Tropic of Cancer – On the Canary Archipelago** a survey is given starting with the Islands' origin up to the present day. This text covers all the islands and is illustrated by the text that follows it, Quotes from 28 Centuries – from Homer to Manrique.

The next big chapter deals solely with **Lanzarote**. The most important themes are covered in short journalistic reports. The small chapter **Places – Sights – Beaches** is in alphabetical order and is meant as a reference source for discovering the island on one's own. Everything that is worth seeing is described in these pages. After that you can find out about **The Canary Cuisine** and translate menus with the help of the Dictionary of Food and Drink. **Special Restaurants** gives you tips where you can eat especially well on the island. **Special Accommodation** mentions the more unusual accommodation available on the island. If you are looking for entertainment, try leafing through **A Brief Survey of Puerto del Carmen. Brief Information on the Island** – ranging from the addresses of doctors and chemists to emergency services to yacht harbours – contains all the information which may be important and necessary or information which is just worth mentioning.

The reference section **General Travel Tips** is valid for all the islands. It is an A–Z directory ranging from air connections to valuable objects. There is also an **Index** to help you find the information you need. We know that a travel guide can never cover everything. We are not able to and don't want to make it suitable for everyone, but we hope that the guide offers the greatest extent of information possible. Things can change after going to press. Lanzarote is going through something of an economic miracle, so things are changing fast, prices above all, so they are not listed here for the most part. Where prices are given – and they are usually approximate – they are merely there as guidelines.

The following information and recommendations were put together by people who know the island very well and who have been living on the Canary archipelago for many years.

First Impressions

Lanzarote is no ordinary island. Formed by volcanic eruptions, this isle is unique and original. The very earth is turned inside out, more than a third of the island is covered by black lava and grey tuff, clinker and volcanic sand. Streams of lava, hardened over the years, but still seemingly fluid in appearance, thread their way through the barren earth. More than 250 years ago Lanzarote experienced the Story of the Creation again. In the Timanfaya National Park, home of the Fire Mountains, are so called "moonscapes". From these one can really get an idea of the "sea of silence" and the powerful forces which are massed and captured beneath the earth's surface. Yet the mountains give a tranquil impression, as though little villages were buried beneath them. Here and in other parts of the island art has been made without artists and the landscape has been sculpted without landscape architects. Nature bequeathed the area with bizarre sculptures, painted the stage sets and wrote its own dramatic script. The island's many contrasts are a constant source of excitement. The whitewashed houses, the black fields covered with *picon* (a volcanic rock and granules of lava), planted with corn and onions. Lime green, yellow, tomato red against a dark background. A dromedary draws the plough, the *magos* (farmers) still harvest together, from field to field. Solitary palm trees, their plams softly curling over to form a shady roof. The softly sloping mountains change their colour according to the light. He who seeks it, can find surrealism "in real life". Natural stone walls thread their way through the planes. Wine and figs thrive in the man made craters (La Geria). It is worth taking a walk along the west

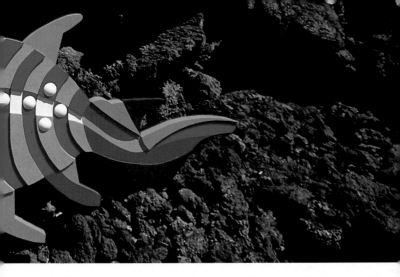

coast. On some days the on shore winds throw up rainbows in the spray. Sharp-sided blocks of magma stand out, giving the impression every now and again of figures. Then there are the white beaches in the south – Papagayo – they are still protected against property development, but the crowds have long since arrived. They are the island's most beautiful beaches. Lanzarote has no woods, very few springs and no ground water. The Harmattan, Sirocco and Levant are all desert winds which have brought sand from the Sahara, which, in turn, creates new deserts. But in earth can flourish. Poppies and daisies and much besides grow after infrequent rain falls (predominantly in winter). He who visits at any time apart from high summer can find surpringly sumptuous vegetation in the north. This is especially surprising for this dry island. Haría is a good example. In the valley of a thousand palm trees, a grove houses a village with a strong Moorish flavour.

Lanzarote possesses elemental force and aesthetic power. The architecture was adapted to the landscape. A solitary tower block in the capital Arrecife acts as a warning against high rise developments. The tourist trade was concentrated on three villages: Puerto del Carmen, Costa Teguise and Playa Blanca. The people of Lanzarote are unassuming, hospitable people; they are slightly reserved, but their reserve has nothing cold about it. They have a happy disposition, one can see that they work hard, that the older people have known deprivation; that makes them tough, but not hard. Lanzarote, known of old as Tyterogakaet, Tyteroygatra or Tarakkaut is the most north easterly, the strangest, most original and impressive island of the whole archipelago of the Canary Islands.

At the Tropic of Cancer

Mythological Background

The Canary Islands. Situated on the Tropic of Cancer. The archipelago of eternal spring. The Elysian Fields. The Garden of the Hesperides. The island of the Saints. According to the tales of Herodotus, in whose time the earth was still thought to be a disc, its edge signalled by violent waves, writhing above seefarers, the point where the world ended and the seas were no longer masterable. Here at the end of the inhabited world; the islands of eternal luck, the "Purpurariae", Atlantis.

Towards the end of the 8th century BC Homer wrote of the Elysian Fields in his Odyssee; these were interpreted as being the Canary Islands. Herodotus (around 490–425/420 BC), the founder of greek historiography, spoke of the Garden of the Hesperides. According to the myth, it was Atlas', the ruler of Mauretania's, cone-shaped mountain which bore the weight of the firmament. Hesperia bore him seven daughters, called the daughters of Atlantis or even the Hesperides. They were banished from the islands, where they are said to have invented night to protect their golden apples from thieves. It was also thought that Plato's (427–347 BC) sunken Atlantis, described in the dialogues "Kritias" and "Timaios", had been discovered here. In the book of Genesis and the book of Ezekiel the Bible calls the islands Elysa or Elysis and the crimson isles. The philosopher and historian Plutarch (around 50–125 BC) spoke of the Islands of the Saints in his "Life of Sertorius". In the year 24 AD the Mauretanian King Juba II

On the Canary Archipelago

sent out an expedition to discover more about these islands shrouded in legends, but the reports of it have been lost. In the texts of the Roman author Elder Pliny (in the first century AD) – who had never actually seen the islands – one finds the first details of the vegetation. He wrote of dragon trees and pine woods. He named the archipelago the "Purpurariae", an allusion to the purple dye the islands produced, just as, long before him around 1100 BC, the Phoenicians had. They set off from Gades, today's Cádiz, on a voyage of discovery along the African coast, came across Lanzarote and Fuerteventura and took from there the Orchilla lichen (*Roccella tinctoria*) from which they gained crimson. The Carthaginians also visited the islands. Despite the numerous visitors, the Canaries were forgotten at the beginning of the early Middle Ages, as early as the 2nd century AD the mathematician, astronomer and geographer Ptolemy (around 85–160 AD) took the island of El Hierro, the island the furthest from the sunset, in the *Punta de Orchilla*, for his prime Meridian. He thus integrated the Canary Islands into the first latitude and longitude grid of the inhabited world and it was only later that the prime meridian was moved to Greenwich. Thus, under the name of *insulae fortunatae* the Canary Islands were part of a world map long before they fell into obscurity.

It is uncertain where today's name for the archipelago comes from. In old writings the island of birds *Canora* (lat. canere – to sing) was mentioned. It is more likely that *Canaria* comes from the tall dogs, which the discoverers found here (lat. canis – dog): thus island of dogs.

Temperatures and Location

The cool Canary stream and the continuous trade winds are responsible for the "everlasting" spring, the mild, settled climate. Pleasant temperatures (average temperature in January 17.5°C, in July 24.2°C) are the norm for both winter and summer; on a latitude so near to the equator much higher temperatures are normal. The Canary Archipelago, the last stop before you cross to America, over 1,600 km north east of the Cape Verde Islands, 1,200 to 1,400 km south east of the Azores, about 1,000 km south west of Gibralter and 500 km south of Madeira, is situated 115 to 500 km away from the coast of North west Africa, by Cape Juby. The archipelago, which is situated on approximately the same degree of latitude as Florida, the Bahamas, the Sahara and Delhi, comprises seven main islands and six smaller islands. They are divided into two groups: The Fortunates: La Palma, El Hierro, La Gomera, Tenerife and Gran Canaria and secondly the Purple Isles Fuerteventura and Lanzarote. Taken as a whole the islands measure 7,499 square km and stretch about 500 km from east to west (between a longitude of 27°38′ and 29°25′ north) and more than 200 km from north to south (between 13°20′ and 18°9′ longitude west. If you catch the passat, so the sailors say anyway, and if you sail unerringly and hard on the wind, you can reach the Panama Canal from here – at the end of which the Galápagos Islands are known to be.

Geological Origin

Are the Canary Islands the remains of a sunken continent? Are they, along with the Azores, the Cape Verde Islands and Madeira the last and thus the highest elevations of Atlantis? Atlantis, which according to Plato was bigger than both Asia and Libya together, is said to have been engulfed by a flood in one night; the flood is said to have been caused by the development of a moon. The theories about the geological origin of the islands are contradictory. Going by current research, the search for Atlantis here seems to be mere illusion. Moreover, the theories that the islands and Africa were once joined by a thin strip of land or that the Canary Islands were situated on a continental crust have not gained credibility. Today it is supposed that the islands are of purely oceanic origin and were never joined to the continent. Parts of a volcanic plug were raised thousands of metres tectonically. The structuring phase, known as the shield phase, lasted half a million years and formed 90% of the land. Fuerteventura and Lanzarote are the oldest islands. They came into being in the middle

Miocene, about 16–20 million years ago. Gran Canaria is thought to have been formed 13–14 million years ago, Tenerife and Gomera about 10 million years ago. La Palma and El Hierro are thought to be about 2–3 million years old. The fall in age from the eastern to the western islands is significant. The drop in age concurs with the theory of plate tectonics which says that the oceanic crust is continuously newly formed by basaltic magma. This is why Europe/Africa and the continent of America have been drifting apart at a rate of 1–2 cm per year for the last 9 million years. The upper mantle, about 400 km thick, is formed predominantly from peridotite stone. The firm lithosphere goes down about 100 km below this. Some scientists presume that the lithosphere moves in an easterly direction to the border area with the aesthenosphere, while magma continuously climbs to the earth's surface from stable chambers in the aesthenosphere. In this way the islands are said to have been formed gradually in a western direction.

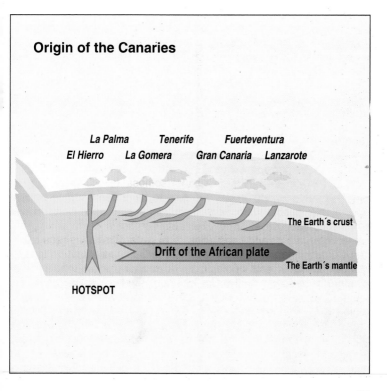

Origin of the Canaries

La Palma   Tenerife   Fuerteventura

El Hierro   La Gomera   Gran Canaria   Lanzarote

The Earth's crust

Drift of the African plate

The Earth's mantle

HOTSPOT

The Ancient Canary People

The first Canary people, the original inhabitants of the archipelago, also known, quite wrongly as *guanches* (*guanches* means sons of Tenerife) were cast up on the islands in about 3000 BC. They probably arrived in primitive boats. Without wanting to. They were probably driven here while fishing off the African coast. They were driven by the Harmattan, the hot Sahara wind, which blows off shore and carries sand and the occasion swarm of grasshoppers with it, blowing in a westerly direction towards the Canary Islands. The Harmattan is accompanied by strong sea currents in the same direction, against which it is impossible to fight in simple boats. Those who went off course and landed on the islands could think of themselves as lucky, although there was no way back. This theory of origin is thought to be tenable by most scientists today, although no sign of water vehicles from that time has ever been found. Even the architect of the fortress, Leonardo Torriani (1590) supposed that the original inhabitants had reached the islands by boat, possibly in dug-out canoes. This is even more astonishing when one considers that, according to the Spanish conquerors, no connections are supposed to have existed between the individual islands until into the 14th century. So the original inhabitants of the Canaries had no experience of boat building or sea travel. (These reports are contradicted by al-Idrisi, the Arab geographer. In his exposition he claims that 1124 Portuguese seafarers reported ships that the first inhabitants had used. Anthropological examinations made on skeletons substantiate a possible connection between the islands before the time of the conquest.)

The Spanish chronicles describe the first Canary people as tall, handsome people, some with blond hair, some with red, all with white skin. The Dominican Fray Alonso Espinosa (1594) praised their qualities in his writings. They are said to have been magnanimous, honourable people who kept their word and who were brave, compassionate, never cruel. He also attributes them with great imaginative talents and unusual spiritual capabilities. The race of the first Canary inhabitants is still part of the Canary population today.

The results of anthropological examinations show that the first inhabitants descended from Cro-Magnon people (wide, earthy face), found in western Ireland, Brittany, the South of France, the Basque region and amongst the Berber tribes of North Africa. (Berbers are white skinned, fair or dark haired). The anthropologist Ilse Schwidetzky thinks that the islands were populated at least twice. About a thousand years prior to our calendar, a second Mediterranean type (with a thin, fine face) landed on the islands. Examinations of mummies and skeletons indicate that the Mediterranean type was taller, superior to the Cromagnides and belonged predominantly to the ruling class.

Comparing language and writing, the researcher Dominik Josef Wölfel (1888–1963) discovered correspondences between the language of the ancient Canary people and North African inscriptions. The spiral stone carvings in the *Cave of Belmaco* on La Palma, the so called megalithic petroglyphs, a "feeling writing", correspond to discoveries in North Africa, West Ireland and, most of all, the spiral carvings on the Brittonian royal grave of King Gravinius. Inscriptions in Hierro show similarities with Libian and Numidian characters from Punic and Roman times in North Africa and the Tifinagh (the characters) of today's Tuareg (according to Wölfel). The *Letreros del Julan* on Hierro contain signs of Cretan linear writing. Schwidetzky and Wölfel assume a common source for both writings; they assume it to be the so-called "westculture". (Westculture is a hitherto unknown high culture, which left traces in the Canary Islands and went into ancient Egyptian and Cretan culture. The writings that were found have nothing to do with actual Egyptian or Cretan culture, but, according to Wölfel, are related to the ancient Mediterranean. They have their origins in the pre- and early dynastic age in Egypt and pre and early Minoan times in Crete.) About 1300 words have been retained from the language of the original inhabitants of the Canary Islands, which, disregarding dialectic differences, had the same origin on all the islands. These words show similarities and uniformities with the language of the Berbers. Some Berbers still live in North Africa, just as the original inhabitants of the Canaries once lived on the archipelago.

The original inhabitants of the Canaries were herdsmen and farmers. They kept mainly sheep, goats and pigs. In the winter they took the herds into the mountains onto the *allmenden* (communally owned pastures). Each tribe possessed a fixed area, often fiercely defended in pastural wars. The arable land was the property of the tribal kings. Families were allocated land for cultivation every year which then reverted to the tribal king after harvest. The size of the plot was determined by the family's standing, the class they belonged to and services to the tribe. The fields were worked upon in groups, which were called *junta* (together) in Gran Canaria, *barranda* or *gallofa* in La Palma. Usually one group went from field to field, irrespective of who owned what, until all fields had been planted. This custom is still carried out in some of the islands today. Just before the rainy season (around the middle of September) the men began to loosen the earth with wooden furrows, the tips of which had goat horns on, while the women sowed the crop. Barley, wheat, peas and broad beans were

grown. After a common harvest the grain was crushed underfoot or with sticks on the *era* (round threshing place). Later the more affluent farmers got their dromedaries and cows to trample the ears of grain, by leading their cattle round and round the era. The staple diet of the first Canary inhabitants was *gofio*, barley meal that was roasted in clay dishes; today it is still part of the Canary diet (although corn or wheat is now used). The preparation of *gofio* involved grinding grains of barley by hand to a fine flour on lava stone. It was then placed in a *zurrón*, a pouch made of goats leather, and mixed to a dough with some water. Sometimes they used the juice of fruit instead of water or mixed in honey for a finer taste. However, the poor could not afford barley. They had to make do with gofio meal made from bracken roots. The animals they kept also provided the Canary people with meat, as well as milk and cheese. They had the animals slaughtered – prisoners were forced to do this "degrading" work. Their meals were enriched with figs, dates, and sea food. There is always a large pile of mussels, so-called *concheros*, near the banks of each island, which bears witness to the great consumption of mussels by its inhabitants. Fish were caught off the coast, without boats and with primitive fishing rods (from wood or bone); they also used lances, fish traps and nets, or more precisely mats that resembled nets, woven out of reeds. In shallow bays – the Canary people could not swim – they drove swarms of fish together. They stunned the fish with the juice of spurge plants, which they shook into the water.

There are plenty of caves and overhanging cliffs of lava and tuff stone on the islands. This meant that the original inhabitants had no accommodation problems. However, strictly speaking, the Canary people were not cave dwellers. If they didn't live in the sparsely furnished caves, then they lived in sheltered ditches or in straw roofed clay huts. This was the case predominantly with the poorer population. They also built huts with skillfully layered walls, built up without mortar. These houses had low doors and small windows and were covered with wooden beams. They covered the beams with straw and laid flat stones (*lajas*) on top of this. Beds were erected from stones; they were also covered in straw, reed mats and animals furs. Mats and animal skins also served as bed covers.

The original Canary inhabitants used tools such as hand mills made from lava which were surprisingly precise, needles and awls made from animal bones and bone gouges, stone knives from Obsidian (*tabonas*), a hard sharp stone glass, also used for arrow heads. They sewed leather purses and the wrapping for mummies, wove reed sacks, carved combs and vessels out of wood and made pottery of very diverse styles considering the small area. Wölfel found correspondences to ancient Egyptian and Nubian ceramics in the Canarian tiefstich ceramics. An individual style of ceramics whose ornament was pressed in to the clay was discovered in La Palma. Wölfel claimed the vessels found in Gran Canaria showed parallels with the Mediterranean and Crete in early Minoan times. The original Canary people wove skirts from reeds and palm leaves; they had no fabric as such. Untanned goat and sheep leather was stitched up with string to form clothes (*tamarcos*), sandals and the emblems of peasant rebels during their insurrections were made from leather. Jewellery, which also served as a method of payment, was made from slices of clay, mussels, stones and bones and strung together on a piece of twine. Wooden javelins, clubs, arrows and catapults, which they deployed surprisingly accurately, were used by the original Canary people as weapons in tribal feuds and battles against the conquerors.

Battles were led by the tribal king. For the warriors, their leader was their very soul. If the king fell, in most cases the warriors became completely weak-willed. The conquerors soon recognized that they only had to gain control of the headman, in order to vanquish the brave heroic warriors. A double kingdom was typical of the Canary Islands. On Tenerife and La Palma the kings were called *menceyes*, on Gran Canaria *guanarteme*. All kings had advisers and headmen (*sigoñe*) at their side, some islands also had priests (*faican*) and women priests who worked as advisers. When Fuerteventura was conquered two senior women ruled alongside many dukes. The first, called *Tamonante*, had a judicial role, the other, *Tibiabin*, who had mediumistic powers, prophetic power and great knowledge, was a female priest. Each tribe had a three class system as its basis; first and foremost king and royal family, then the aristocracy, then the people. Members of the lowest class could be promoted to the aristocracy if they showed special merit. Only a man of whom no one could say they had seen him milk or kill his goat, steal in peacetime, prepare his own meals, or behave unrespectfully, especially towards women, could be knighted. However, if anyone at the ceremony could claim anything to the contrary, the candidate was relegated to being a common soldier until the end of his days, was completely shorn and was called from then on *trasquilado* (the shorn one). Women from the lower orders could probably only reach the aristocracy by marrying. The wives of the king or the headman had to be aristocratic. Because of this, inter-family marriages were common. The king's elder brother and then the king's son were next in line to the throne. In Tenerife every kingdom had a living and a dead king. The relic elevated the dead man to the status of a still ruling king.

Toasting corn for gofio

Queso de cabra

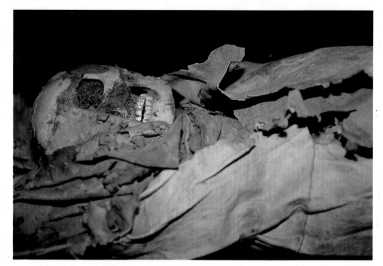

Canarian mummy

The Caves at Cenobio de Valerón

The marital customs of the original Canarians left them with great personal freedom. If two people wanted to marry, the partners will was sufficient. In the same way a declaration of will by one of the partners was enough to end the marriage. There was no obstacle to getting married again. However, the children of a separated marriage were disadvantaged; they were regarded as illegitimate. There is still debate as to whether the women of Gran Canaria and Lanzarote were married to three or four men, who alternated every month in their role as man of the house and beneficiary of marital rights.

Every island had a different system of penal law. On Fuerteventura the criminal's skull was smashed in with a stone. The "Sons of Tenerife" were unusually mild. The murderer was relieved of his property (which was given to dependants as compensation), and was then chased out of the kingdom. On Hierro the price paid for theft was an eye. On La Palma, however, theft was regarded as an art.

The original Canary people on all islands believed in a single, almighty, good god by the name of *Abora*, *Acuhurajan* or *Althos* (all three words mean great). *Abora* was the counterpart to *Guayota*, an evil god. He was believed to live in the crater of the Teide on Tenerife and avenge the evil deeds of people with volcanic eruptions. On circularly constructed places of sacrifice at the foot of volcanoes, the faithful tried to appease *Guayota* with gifts. Consecrated virgins, the *harimaguadas*, who dedicated themselves to the service of *Abora* lived in the caves in the mountains. After a few years of abstinence they were allowed to leave the women's order and get married. The kings and aristocrats had first pick of the virgins. The best known monastery is the site of *Cenobio de Valerón* on Gran Canaria. 297 caves served as monastic cells and granaries; they were joined in seven and more floors by galleries and stairs. Priestesses had the task of asking for rain and, in times to catastrophe, for *Abora's* protection. The priests, on the other hand, took on a judicial role and acted as a mediator in great quarrels.

The cult of the dead of the original Canary people is reminiscent of the culture of ancient Egypt. The corpses of the upper class were mummified. The innards were removed, but never the brain, all orifices of the body were sealed with bees wax and the body was rubbed with a mixture of animal fats, the sap of the dragon tree, aromatic herbs, resins, tree bark and crushed pumice stone. The drying out process lasted several weeks. The mummies were subsequently sewed into goat and sheeps skin, laid in dug-out tree trunks and buried upright in caves. The mummies had no bandages as was customary in Egypt since the Canarians could not weave. A mummie wrapped in goat's leather can be viewed in the Canary Museum in Las Palmas de Gran Canaria. Members of the lower classes were not mummyfied, but just buried in caves. Tumulus burials are also known from Gran Canaria (tumulus means prehistoric sepulchral mound). This is mainly represented by single graves. The dead man was laid in a dug out grave and the ground was covered in stones. The big tumulus of La Guancha at Gáldar is still noteworthy. It contains over thirty burials and is estimated to date back to 1082 AD. Due to its climatic conditions, Gáldar was a rich area and the seat of the royal dynasty *Andamanas*, along with the high aristocracy. It is possible that the great tumulus was the grave of this clan.

Apart from natural catastrophes and occasional attacks by slave dealers or pirates, the original Canary people lived for hundreds of years in peace and quiet, forgotton by the rest of the world, engrossed in a stone age culture with little sign of change, without knowing about the invention of the wheel and without metal mineral resources. They lived in peace – that is until the Christians came. The "abandoned" islands found notice once more. And every piece of land where the inhabitants were not Christian was also regarded as "abandoned". In the 14th century the Spanish conquerors showed the original inhabitants what Christian civilisation and brotherly love meant. Under the auspices of the Bible they held in front of them, they struck dead all those who didn't submit. The same fate befell the original inhabitants of the Canary Islands as was to befall the Indian Americans. The conquest of the Canary Islands was a dishonourable and gruesome massacre which took the majority of the original inhabitants as its victims.

Rediscovery and Conquest

The Canary Islands were next discovered by Genoan seefarers in 1292. However, Europeans only developed a real interest in the islands at the beginning of the 14th century. In 1312 the Genoan Lanzelot Maloisel, known as Lanzarotto Malocello, landed on the most north easterly island Tyteroygatra (named by the original inhabitants). This island was probably named Lanzarote after him. In 1341 the Portuguese king dispatched three war ships which landed on Gran Canaria. Their five month long occupation of a coastal strip proceeded with great losses. With little booty, but taking five Canarians, the unsuccessful conquerors sailed back to Portugal. Between 1340 and 1342 the islands were plagued by Portuguese, Spaniards, Mallorcans out to catch slaves and involved in robbery.

Casa de Colon

The nobleman Luis de la Cerda – Count of Talmot, feudal lord of Oléron and of la Mothesur Rhône, Admiral of France, son of the disherited King without land, Alphons of Castile and grandson of Alphons X of Castile – was crowned king of the Canary Islands in 1344 in Avignon by Pope Clemens VI – the head of all countries still to be discovered. For a yearly payment of 400 golden florins to the Roman church, de la Cerda was given the kingdom which he believed he had been cheated out of. Luis de la Cerda never conquered his kingdom. Even an expedition there seemed too dangerous for him. He merely had to defend his distant kingdom against the demands of Portugal and Castile.

Henry III of Castile inherited the islands and nominated Roberto de Bracamonte as de la Cerda's successor. Like his predecessor, Bracamonte could make little of his title. Bracamonte actually did keep the title, but appointed his nephew, the Norman nobleman and knight Jean de Béthencourt (1359–1426) – who had fallen out of favour with his own King Charles IV – to conquer the islands. In 1402 Béthencourt, together with the Spanish nobleman Gadifer de la Salle (1340–1422), set sail from La Rochelle for the islands. Once they had landed on Lanzarote they converted the chieftain *Guadarfía* and his subjects quickly to Christianity. The natives were saved from slavery by their conquest. For the first time the Spanish crown possessed one of the Canary Islands. In the same year Béthencourt returned to Spain to request means and reinforcements to conquer the other islands. The diplomat installed the actual conqueror of the islands and warrior La Salle as his representative and governor on Lanzarote. At court in Seville Béthencourt concealed La Salle's victories from Henry III and increased his own excessive levy; this brought him the title of "Lord of the Islands". When La Salle, who had also harboured hopes of the title, heard of Béthencourt's misdemeanours, he returned to France in bitter resentment. In 1405 the people of Fuerteventura surrendered. This conquest was described by Béthencourt as a *"great adventure"* (*fuerte ventura*). In Fuerteventura he founded his capital Betancuria, where the first episcopal church of the archipelago was founded in 1424. He also conquered Hierro, which fell to him through betrayal. *Armiche*, the ruler of Hierro, trusted the word of Béthencourt who had suggested peace talks. The island prince surrendered with 111 of his subjects. Béthencourt seized hold of these original inhabitants and distributed them like animals amongst his people, some were even sold as slaves. Although he has often been accredited with having done so, he was not able to conquer Gomera. Gomera was still counted as the property of the Béthencourts. They sold estates to aristocrats under a feudal system. Attempts to conquer Gran Canaria and La Palma failed. In 1406 Béthencourt returned to Europe and gave the affairs of the crown over to his nephew Maciot de Béthencourt who ruled until 1415 as viceroy. He ruled unscrupulously and brutally. He lined his own pockets quite indiscriminatingly until finally on the instigation of the Spanish King he was forced to give up his office. In 1418 he sold his office directly on to several people. He sold to the regal envoy Diego de Herrera, to Prince Henry of Portugal and to the Spanish Count Hernán Peraza the Elder. Hernán Peraza the Younger took over the rule. His heir(ess) Doña Inés – married to Diego García de Herrera – continued the corrupt feudalism until the catholic King Ferdinand of Aragon and Isabella of Castile ended the privileges of the aristocracy, by setting the islands under the power of the Crown. However, the property laws remained unclear. The Portuguese, for their part, also made claims to the archipelago. A contest between the two royal houses had begun. Attempted conquests by the Portuguese lasted from 1420 to 1479. On Gomera they could assert themselves without subjugating the natives. In the treaties of Alcácovas and Toledo (1479) the two parties came to an agreement: Castile was entitled to pursue the conquest of the whole of the Canary archipelago, while Portugal's supremacy in North West Africa and Guinea was recognised. Colonisation could begin.

In the name of the Castilian crown, Juan Rejón founded Las Palmas de Gran Canaria as early as 1478. Bloody clashes had raged with the original inhabitants for five years. They only came to an end when the Spanish were able to entice the *guanarteme* of Telde, *Doramas* into an ambush, kill him and hang his head out for display. The resistance of *Doramas'* subjects was over. The second king, *Artemi Semidan*, *guanarteme* of Gáldar, was transported to Spain where he was baptized. Even though the original inhabitants of Gran Canaria rebelled again and again, the conquistadores celebrated surrender on 29 April 1483. In 1488 Gomera fell, in 1496 La Palma. By the end of the same year the Spanish also had the upper hand on Tenerife.

The aristocratic Andalusian of Galician descent Alonso Fernández de Lugo and the conquistador Pedro de Vera broke the resistance on Gran Canaria and La Palma. After months of fighting they offered the Canary people a cease-fire. The Spaniard's lack of dignity again became evident: they broke their word and took the leader, Prince *Tanausú*, captive on his way to negotiations. At this point, as on Gran Canaria, the original inhabitants surrendered. *Tanausú* brought his life to an end with a hunger strike. On Tenerife the *guanches* were able to defend themselves more successfully at first. Admittedly, the nine ruling *menceyes* were constantly feuding so that the *mencey* of Güimar, *Añaterve* allied himself with Lugo against the other chieftains, yet the *guanches* inflicted a painful defeat upon the Spaniards. The *guanches* were led by *mencey Bencomo* of Taoro (Orotava Valley) and his brother *Tinguaro*. In spite of their superior weapons, over 1000 Spaniards fell in 1494 near today's village of La Matanza de Acentejo (the slaughter of Acentejo). A year later, in a last battle, the *guanches*, weakened by a European plague which the conquistadores had brought in, were devastatingly defeated near La Victoria de Acentejo (the victory of Acentejo). A year later the last *mencey* surrendered. From now on the Spanish had the archipelago firmly in their grasp. There is still an independence movement today, which a strong minority of the Canary people belong to.

Colonisation

In 1496 de Lugo founded the city of La Laguna on Tenerife as the royal seat and administrative capital. The Spaniards seized hold of the fertile valleys in the north of Tenerife and drove the *guanches*, the actual owners of the land, to the barren south. In the following period the original population was integrated into the class of the Spanish conquerors – as long as they weren't sold off as slaves, that is. Spaniards married Canary women. Over the next centuries the peoples interbred.

La Palma, Gran Canaria and Tenerife, the profitable "green" islands were directly under the authority of the Spanish crown after the conquest. They were called *islas realengas* (the royal islands). The *capitanes generales* (general captains), the military commanders of the provinces, possessed the highest authority, together with the leading representatives of the catholic church. The general captains gave out the usufructs for the land and sold the water rights. Gomera, Hierro, Fuerteventura and Lanzarote, the "dry" islands, were also under the authority of the crown, but also received *señorio* status; that is the property rights were given to the aristocracy and clergy, the *señoriales*, the feudal lords. Their land was tended by slaves and bondsmen or was leased out to *medianeros*. The owner and the leaseholder shared the net profit exactly between them (*en medio*). Sugar cane plantations were planted, trade was done with wine and pot herbs. Travellers to America stopped off here, the first riches were gained. It was primarily the foreigners who pocketed the profit. They possessed the water rights, the land, the plantations and some of the ports. Speculating Italians, Spaniards, Dutchmen, Englishmen and Frenchmen were the major participants in the "capital investment" of the Canary Islands. The original Canary inhabitants and their country were relentlessly exploited. The *godos*, the exploiters, who were already rich, became richer; the majority of the original inhabitants of the Canaries, however, remained poor. The sums they invested were always lower than the sums that the speculators and tradesmen transferred abroad. In 1537 the Spanish crown finally banned slave trade. Despite this, the profiteering conquerors repeatedly broke this ban. A recent decree by Pope Paul III made slave trading punishable.

The Canary Islands won increasingly in strategic and economic importance; more and more ships stopped in their ports. Hundreds of visitors visited the islands, some of them undesirable. Pirates were attracted by the promise of a keen booty, the archipelago became a renewed target for conquests. In 1599 a Dutch fleet landed off Gomera. After England had won authority of the seas, they repeatedly tried to capture the islands for their empire. In 1657 the attack by Admiral Blake was fended off. During the Spanish War of Succession the attempt by Admiral Genning, who in 1704 occupied Gibralter for England, to conquer Santa Cruz de Tenerife failed. In 1797 Admiral Horatio Nelson, who later won at Trafalgar over the Franco-Spanish fleet, threatened Santa Cruz with a fleet of eight war ships. With his crew of 1,200 he at first succeeded in going ashore. However, when the defending army received reinforcements and aimed their fire at the ships, Nelson was forced to weigh the anchor and turn about. The Spaniards sunk the auxiliary cruiser Fox and its crew of 200. In this act of conquest, the victory veteran Nelson was hit by a bullet. Using a saw and much rum for anaesthetization his right arm was amputated. It was only after Nelson had signed a pact of non attack with his left hand that the commander of the Spanish fortress Antonio Gutiérrez released the English prisoners. The El Tigre cannon in the harbour of Santa Cruz is still today a memory of Nelson's only capitulation. Santa Cruz de Tenerife had already become the administrative capital in place of La Laguna in 1723. In 1778 it was given the privilege of being able to trade with America.

Castillo San Gabriel

Into the 20th Century

In spite of their strategically favourable situation, events of world history in the 19th century made no impact on the Canary Islands. In 1822 Santa Cruz de Tenerife was made into the capital of the whole archipelago. In 1837 the *señorio*-status was abandoned on Gomera, Hierro, Lanzarote and Fuerteventura. In 1852 the Spanish queen Isabella II made the Canaries into a free port zone. Towards the end of the 19th century the export-oriented banana production became the main branch of the economy. In 1912 the *cabildos insulares* were created; a local self governing body, a form of state parliament for each island. And in 1927 the archipelago was divided into two provinces; the province of Santa Cruz de Tenerife with the islands Tenerife, Gomera, Hierro and La Palma, and the province of Las Palmas de Gran Canaria, with Gran Canaria, Fuerteventura and Lanzarote. Both provinces formed a communal military area under the control of General Francisco Franco. In 1936 in the Esperanza wood on Tenerife he gathered together the leading officers and called for a "national uprising" against the Republicans. This resulted in the Spanish Civil

War in which German socialists and communists fought on the side of the Republicans whilst Franco was supported by Hitler's troops. The Civil War raged for three years ending in victory for Franco. Franco remained the dictator of Spain until his death in 1975. On 22 November of the same year King Juan Carlos took over power as the head of state. In a parliamentary monarchy the parliament, the Cortes, adopted a new constitution in 1978. Spain became a consitutional monarchy. Five years later the Canary Islands, like the other sixteen "Autonomous Regions", received a regional constitution (statute of autonomy) and elected representative bodies. Spain's membership of the European Community followed on 1 January 1986. However, the Canary Islands won a special status.

Tourism on the Canary Islands holds a special place today. Contributing 67% to the gross national product, it is the most important branch of the economy on the archipelago. Since 1955, when the fishing village of Puerto de la Cruz on Tenerife began to develop into one of the leading tourist spots in the world, tourism has grown constantly – with only occasional breaks.

Christopher Columbus

Quotes from 28 Centuries

"But you, O beloved of Zeus, Meneleus, are not fated
To die in the steed feeding Argos,
You will be led by the Gods once to the ends of the earth,
Into the Elysian Chamber, where the burnished hero Radamanthus
Lives and peaceful life is the constant comfort of mankind:
(No snow is found there, no winter hurricane, no pouring rain,
Eternal blow the rustlings of the lightly breathing West,
Sent by the Ocean to softly cool humanity) ..."
HOMER, The Odyssee, 8th century BC

There are two of them, divided from one another by a very narrow stretch of sea, ten thousand leagues from Africa; they are called the Islands of the Saints. Watered only infrequently by mighty falls of rain, mostly by gentle dew-bringing winds, they offer not only a good and sumptuous land for tilling and planting, but also bear exotic fruits, sufficient in quantity and taste to feed an idle people without work and troubles. The climate on the islands is very pleasant resulting from the mixture and hardly noticeable change of seasons. The North and East winds blowing from our part of the world scatter when they reach this breadth of endless space and become weaker; the sea winds blowing up from the South and East sometimes bring mighty rain storms from the sea, but mostly they shower the islands with a moist breeze which makes them fertile. It is for this reason that the firm belief has spread as far as the Barbarians that this is the home of the Elysian Fields and the Saints, about which Homer had waxed lyrical.

PLUTARCH, Comparative Descriptions of Life: Sertorius, 1./2. century AD

"(. . .) Today we were able to put into Gran Canaria. I was frustrated in my hope of replacing the "Pinta" by another ship. So we have no option but to try and get a new rudder made. Pinzón thinks he will manage it. I would also like to replace the triangular sails of the "Niña" with round ones, so that the ship can work more securely and won't have to stay behind.

For the seefarer there is no greater enemy than superstition. As we passed Tenerife we were able to observe a volcanic eruption in process. The smoke and the flames, the glowing masses of lava, the muffled din coming from the earth innards, put the crew into a panic-ridden dread. A bad omen – what else? I told them of Etna and other volcanoes, but my words fell on deaf ears. They believed that the volcano had only erupted because we were making this trip.

I was certainly concerned about this, but even more disturbed by the news that a ship coming from Ferro" (Hierro today) "brought. Apparently there are three Portuguese caravels at sea with the task of taking me captive and bringing my expedition to an end. The passage from La Rábida to Córdoba is long and that from Palos to Lisbon even longer. Nevertheless, the King of Portugal knows very well that I have gone to sea. He no longer needs me, now that Diaz has found the Eastern passage to India; nevertheless he wants to deny me the western passage. If I succeed – and I will succeed – in winning the seas and reaching areas where no other dares to go, Joao's caravels will return to Lisbon empty handed. Time which previously always

passed too quickly, is now passing too slowly. The "Pinta" will not be sea worthy for another three weeks."
CHRISTOPHER COLUMBUS, Log-book, 9 August 1492

"There are two wheat harvests, one in February and one in May. The grain is uncommonly good and produces bread which is as white as snow. (...) This island produces particularly fine wine, predominantly in the town of Telde, and particular sorts of good fruits, the best of which is definitely the plantano. The tree provides no domestic wood; it grows near to the streams, the stalks are very thick and it has an extrordinarily thick foliage which grows not from the branches, but from the top of the tree. Every leaf is two cubits long, and almost half a cubit wide. Each tree has only two or three branches and on these the fruit grows – thirty or forty more or less at a time. The fruit looks like a cucumber; when it is ripe it is completely black and much tastier than any preservative. This island is also the home of many oxen, cows, camels, goats, sheep, capons, hens, ducks, doves and partridges. Wood is the thing which is missing most."
THOMAS NICOLS, Description of the Canary Isles, around 1560

"It is only in the last 120 or 140 years that the Canary people have known illness; they lived without knowing or feeling it before. If this state of health can be attributed to the completeness and mildness of the air, the reason for it must also lie much more in their little varying and complimentary diet; they feed on only barley, cooked, steamed or roast fish, milk and butter – substances which are good for human health. (...) Since the Canarians have been living in peace under the rules of kings, they have begun to build houses and settlements together and have got used to living in an urban environment abandonning their lives as farmers and herdsmen. (...) The Canary people also built houses in the caves of mountains or dug out the tuff or solid earth – all this without wood or iron or other tools apart from goats bones and very hard stones which could cut the finest and sharpest steel. They made the stones so fine and smooth that they could even use them to bleed themselves and they are currently used by farmers in Canaria as razor blades, called Tavas, just as they were once named. (...) Amongst these Canary people there were three types of fights for which they had three different sorts of weapons. The first two are mentioned above, the third was those thin stones called tavas they used for cutting and bleeding themselves. They used these to injure each other when they fought breast to breast.

When two Canarians challenged each other to a fight, they went to the appointed place, a small raised area with a flat stone on either side, just big enough for a man to stand upon. Firstly, each man stood upon his stone with three pebbles in his hand to throw at the other, those three stones used for injuries and with the stick called a Magodo and Amodeghe. First of all they threw the stones at each other, which they skillfully avoided without moving their feet. Next they stepped down onto the ground and encountered each other with clubs, each one fencing and looking for an advantage, in the usual style of fighting. And then, in the full fury of the fight, if it came to a scuffle, they used the three sharp stones which they had between the fingers of their left hand to injure one another. And then one of them proclaimed himself beaten by the other by crying in a loud voice "gamá, gamá" meaning "no more, no more", upon which the victor stopped fighting and the two became friends with each other."
LEONARDO TORRIANI, The Canary Isles and Their Original Inhabitants, 1590

"Anderson, the natural scientist on Captain Cook's third expedition, advises European doctors to send their patients to Tenerife – not because some healers perversely choose the most remote resorts, but much more to do with the extrordinarily mild and even climate in the Canaries. The island is built like an ampitheatre and, as with Peru and Mexico, although in smaller measures, displays a range of climates from African heat to the frost of the high Alps. Santa Cruz, the port of Orotava, the town of the same name and Laguna are four places where the middle temperatures decrease respectively. Southern Europe does not offer the same advantages, for the change of seasons makes itself much too noticeable. Tenerife, on the other hand, both the gateway to the Tropics and just a few days journey from Spain, displays a great deal of the natural magnificence found in countries between the tropics. Several of the most beautiful and splendid forms of the vegetable kingdom can be found here, bananas and palms. He who has an eye for the beauty of nature, can find an even more powerful means of convalescence than the climate. No other place in the world seems more suited to me to rid melancholy and restore peace to a deeply troubled nature than Tenerife and Madeira. (...)

Date palms and coconut trees adorn the banks of the sea; high up above, bushes of bananas stand out against dragon trees, whose trunks really do reveal a snake's body. The slopes are planted with vines which entwine themselves around very high trellises. Orange trees covered in blossom, myrtles and cypress trees surround chapels, erected on free-standing hills with reverence. Everywhere property is enclosed by hedgerows of agave and cactus. Numerous cryptogamic plants, especially ferns, clothe the walls, which are kept moist by little clear springs of water. In winter, when the volcano is covered with snow and ice, one can enjoy an eternal Spring in this part of the country. (...)

Climbing the volcano of Tenerife is not just attractive because it offers such rich material for scientific research, but rather because it offers he who has a sense for the greatness of nature a wealth of pictorial splendour. (...) On the top of it one not only gains a magnificent view right across the sea, stretching over the highest mountains of the neighbouring islands, but one can also see the forests of Tenerife and inhabited strips of coastal land which appear so near that the outlines and colours stand out in the most glorious contrasts. We settled ourselves at first on the outside edge of the crater and looked north westerly where the coast is dotted with villages and hamlets. Pockets of mist, swirling continuously around our feet, driven by the wind, offered us the most diverse spectacle. An even layer of cloud between us and the lowest regions of the island was punctuated here and there by little streams of air, sent up by the earth's surface warmed by the sun. The port of Orotava, the ships anchored there, the gardens and vineyards around the town were made visible through these openings, which promised to open up at any moment. From these remote regions we looked down upon the inhabited world; we took delight in lively contrast between the arid flanks of the volcano, its steep slopes covered in clinker, its plateau, void of all vegetation, and the laughing sight of the developed land; we saw how the vegetation divided itself into zones according to the decreasing temperatures as the height rose. Beneath the piton lichen begins to spread over the clogged, gleaming lava, a species of violet (viola cheiranthifolia), closely related to the viola decumbens, grows along the slope of the volcano to a height of 3,390 meters. Blossoming retama bushes adorn the small valleys, ravaged by rain storms and blocked up by secondary side eruptions. Below the Ratama the area of ferns begins, below this grows tree-like heather. Woods of laurel trees, rhamnus and strawberry trees are situated between the heather and areas planted with vines and fruit trees. A carpet of rich green spreads its way from the areas of gorse and alpine herbs up to the groups of date palms, muses, their feet seemingly lapped by the ocean.

The fact that the villages, vineyards and gardens seem so close from the top of the volcano, has a lot to do with astonishing clearness of the air. In spite of the considerable distance, we could recognise houses, tree trunks, the ships' rigging; we could also see the rich vegetation of the planes in the livliest colour. The splendour of the landscape below the tropics is based on this clearness; it accentuates the gloss of the colours in the vegetation and increases the magical effect of their harmonies and contrasts.

We extended our stay on the top of the volcano, waiting in vain for the moment in which we would be able to see the whole archipelago of blissful islands. At our feet we saw Palma, Gomera, and Gran Canaria. The mountains of Lanzarote which had been free of cloud at dawn, soon shrouded themselves again in thick clouds.

The cold temperature that we experienced on the top of the volcano, was very significant for the time of year. In the shadow the thermometer showed 2,7 degrees Celsius. The wind was from the west – that is from the contrary direction to the wind that blows hot air over Tenerife for a large part of the year and which rises up over the burning deserts of Africa."

ALEXANDER VON HUMBOLDT, From Orinoco to the Amazon, 1889

"The world lives from the Islands"
CÉSAR MANRIQUE, 20th century

About Lanzarote

The Naming of Lanzarote

Even in ancient times the Tabaiba bush (Euphorbia regis-jubae) grew on Lanzarote. A healing drink was brewed from it. The Romans are said to have known the bush under the name of Sarcocolla (fishlime). In old Spanish Sarcocolla means "Laçarotes". However, it is not certain whether this is the reason why the island has today's name. One legend attributes the naming of Lanzarote to the Norman nobleman Jean de Béthencourt, who landed there in 1402. When he experienced no resistance from the Canarians on his arrival, he is said to have broken his lance in two and cried "¡Lanza rota!" (lance broken). However, Béthencourt is also said to have spoken Spanish and so it is thought he would not have needed to express himself in such banal terms. The prevailing opinion is that the island was probably named after the Genoan Lanzarotto Malocello who rediscovered the island in 1312.

Historical Background

Little has been written down about the history of Lanzarote. The search for sources only brings sketchy material. This has not least to do with the numerous volcano eruptions which destroyed villages and the archives which they contained.

The first detailed reports appear after 1312 when Lanzarotto Malocello landed on the island. The original inhabitants whom he found there, predominantly of the Cro-Magnon race, had been visited by various seafarers since ancient times. In spite of the many attacks by pirates which they had to tolerate, they showed great hospitality. It is presumably due to this hospitality that there were never any devastating battles between the conquistadores and the ancient Canarians on Lanzarote.

The people of ancient Lanzarote were part of a principality which stretched across the whole island. In contrast to the other islands, where hostile tribes fought among themselves, the people of Lanzarote held together. Most women – so it is said – had three to four husbands who alternated on a monthly basis. The next in turn worked as servant in the house the woman shared with her current partner.

In 1377 the Spaniard Martin Ruiz de Avendaño landed. As a sign of his hospitality, the ruling King Zonzamas put his beautiful wife Fayna at his disposition; she bore Avendaño the legendary Princess Icó. Zonzama's son Tiguafaya succeeded him; he was later captured by slave handlers together with his wife and numerous tribesmen. Guanarame, another son of Zonzama married his half-sister Icó. Icó claimed that their son, Guadarfía, should succeed to the throne. Legend tells how she was put to a smoke test without which the other tribesmen refused to recognize Guadarfía's rights. Icó was walled into Zonzamas's grave with three servants and the grave was filled with smoke. If she suffocated, then her low origin was proven. However, a cunning old woman had advised her to breathe through a dampened sponge which eliminated the smoke. Icó survived and Guadarfía acceeded to the throne.

In 1402 Jean de Béthencourt conquered Lanzarote. This was the start of the conquest of the other islands. It is presumed that Béthencourt, who landed in Southern Lanzarote with a crew of 63 men, met Guadarfía. Béthencourt and the island prince made a pact. The Spaniards were obliged to build a fort against attackers – like pirates and slave traders – while Guadarfía surrendered himself and his people, as he noted, "as a friend, but not as a subject". The fort was discovered under the sand near the now deserted village of Papagayo, along with the chapel of San Marcial which the conquerors also erected. Today San Marcial is the patron saint of the island.

In 1402, while Béthencourt had returned to Seville to request ammunition and reinforcements for the conquest of the other islands, the previously large population is said to have been decimated to about 300 by pirate attacks and slave catchers. In 1405 Béthencourt conquered Fuerteventura from Lanzarote. Lanzarote fell into the hands of the Count of Niebla and the Herrera-Peraza family, who governed Lanzarote as feudal lords. The distribution of large areas of land that took place at that time is still in effect today, with just a few exceptions. The system of feoffment was abolished in 1837. Despite the fact that Lanzarote was able to avoid a battle at its conquest, peace still evaded the island. In addition to volcanic eruptions and periods of drought there were repeated attempted conquests and attacks by slave dealers and pirates. Five extreme droughts, which each lasted more than two years, in the middle of the 16th and 19th century, deprived the people of Lanzarote of even the basics of life. From 1703–1779 the people suffered a continued famine. Lanzarote (and Fuerteventura) were almost depopulated. The inhabitants of these islands fled to Gran Canaria and Tenerife. Many died. Refusing to give up, some returned to their homeland and started a basic existence again there.

Geography

Lanzarote lies between the 28th and 30th degree of nothern latitude and the 13th and 14th degree of western longitude. Situated 115 km from the west coast of Africa, Lanzarote stretches over 62 km from the Punta de Papagayo in the South to the Punta Fariones in the North. It is 21 km wide. About 60,000 inhabitants populate an area of 795 square km (the same area as Hamburg) – a medium density of population of approximately 75 inhabitants per square km. If one disregards the uninhabitable wilderness around the volcano, which claims about a third of the whole area (260 square km), a middling density of population of 112 inhabitants per square km emerges. For comparison the population density of other places (all figures are approximate): Fuerteventura 14; West Germany 246; England 361; Norway 13; Spain 77. Around 30,000 people live in the capital Arrecife. Only about 30% of the land is cultivated and of economic value. In the west and north of the island the coastline is rugged, whilst the east and south coast offer white beaches which are good for bathing and water sports. The highest peak in Lanzarote is the Peñas del Chache in the Famara mountain range in the north; it is 671 m high. In the south the Atalaya stands out 608 m above sea level. It is the "local mountain" of Femés. From the top of the Atalaya, when the weather is clear, one can see over the whole island, which is home to more than 100 volcanoes and more than 300 craters. One also has a complete view of the "volcano wildnerness", which, measuring 260 square metres, makes up approximately one third of the whole area of Lanzarote. This is the site of the Timanfaya range of mountains incorporating the Montañas del Fuego (the Fire Mountains). The Islote de Hilario is the last "active" volcano. This third of the island has been made into a national park. Timanfaya is also the name of a village which was submerged beneath volcanic eruptions. The period of eruptions lasted a long time and went on into the 19th century.

Volcanic Eruptions in the 18th and 19th Century

The mightiest eruptions in volcanic history took place on Lanzarote between 1730 and 1736. In this period of time George Washington, first president of the USA and James Watt, the English inventor of the modern steam engine were born, Bach composed his mass in B-minor, Handel his concerti grossi; Gottsched wrote his "Suggestions Towards a Critical Poetics for the Germans", Voltaire his French drama "Zaïre", the 1,062 km long canal between Petersburg (the Baltic Sea) and Wolga (the Caspian Sea) was started (finished 1799) and Hadley drew up his theory of the trade winds. The world only learnt of the monstrous catastrophe on Lanzarote much later. Far away from busy Europe, the pastor of Yaiza, Don Andres Lorenzo Curbelo, witnessed the eruptions at first hand:

"On the first September of 1730 between nine and ten in the evening, the earth suddenly erupted. In the region of Timanfaya a mighty mountain rose up from beneath the earth's surface. Flames

shot up and burned for nineteen days on end (...). A few days later a new maw opened up and furious streams of lava were spat out onto Timanfaya, Rodeo and a part of the Mancha Blanca. The lava streamed across the villages, at first swirling and rapid like water, then heavy and glutinous like honey. With a mighty roar rock emerged from within the volcano and changed the direction of the flow of lava. Now it no longer flowed towards the north, but in a westerly direction. It reached the villages of Macetas and Santa Catalina and completely crushed them under its flow. (...) On the 2nd of September 1731 the lava made a further violent attack. It rained down on Mazo, burned and buried the village and plunged, like a fiery cataract and with the most hideous din, into the sea. This went on for eight days. After this everything became quiet again and it seems as though the eruptions were at an end. But on the 18th October three new mouths broke out directly above the cindered Santa Catalina, emitting clouds of smoke which covered the whole island. They carried ash with them. Heavy drops of rain fell over the whole island. Darkness, ash and smoke drove the inhabitants of Yaiza and the surroundings away more than once. They returned, however, since no further destruction followed

the explosion. Ten days after this explosion the cattle in the entire district fell dead. It had suffocated on the stinking smog. From the 1st to the 20th November smoke and ash were continuously catapulted from the craters. And on the 27th November a stream of lava whirled down the mountain with incredible rapidity. On the 1st of December it reached the sea. Setting as it cooled, it formed an island surrounded by dead fish. On the 16th of December the lava unexpectedly changed direction; instead of running into the sea it now ran in a south westerly direction burning the community of Chupadero and subsequently devastating the fertile plain of Uga. There the lava stopped and cooled. On the 7th of January 1732 new eruptions devoured the old craters. (...)"

The previously fertile land, once known as the granary of Lanzarote, was buried beneath metres of volcanic material in unimaginable quantities. The good people of Lanzarote waited in fright and dread for many days. They hoped that the volcanic eruptions would soon be over. But "on the 25th of December the earth shook more violently than before and three days later the village of Jaretas was burned out by lava and the chapel of St John was destroyed" (Curbelo). Now the people gave up the hope that the island could ever come to peace. Led by their pastor, some of them fled to Gran Canaria, others to Fuerteventura and Tenerife. A decree by Philipp V forbade the people of Lanzarote, under the threat of death, to leave the island. So some of them remained on the fire-spewing island. When

the earth finally came to peace on the 16th April 1736, a third of Lanzarote was wasteland. Streams of lava had flooded over the plains of Tomara, destroying twelve villages and crushing 420 houses in all. Scarcely ninety years later, in 1824, the earth erupted for what is until now the last time. The fertile plains of Tiagua disappeared, devoured by streams of lava. These eruptions were not as extensive as those of the 18th century, but they were nevertheless dangerous. The lava was extremely thin and fluid and careered down the valley with great speed.

This "moon landscape" is unique and is a treasure trove for geologists. All the different manifestations of volcanic activity can be seen side by side. Despite the keen research which has been carried out, scientists are still unable to explain why the last two phases of volcanic activity are separated by millions of years.

The Population

The island and its population is often brought into association with the rabbit: *isla conejera* (conejo – rabbit; conejera – rabbit warren). The natives call themselves *conejeros*, very roughly translated as rabbit hunter. As on all the Canary Islands, people address each other by Christian name. In the constant battle against nature, they formed a tough and taciturn kind of people who knew how to cultivate the barren earth with their hands, the dromedary and the Roman plough and with trouble and hard work managed to reap the bare essentials from it. (see Cultivation of Unirrigated Land, p.59) Dressed in black and wearing the typical black felt hat, one can still occasionally spot the *mago* (farmer) drawing the plough, while the women sow the crops or plant onions in their ankle-length dresses. The Lanzarotenos are a people made up from ancient Canary and Spanish influences; every now and again Moorish traits can be seen in the inhabitants, as well as an Egyptian, Berber or Normanic influence; a touch of the Viking can also be seen in the many Canary people with red-blond hair. The difference between the Cro-Magnon and Mediterranean type can still be seen today. The people of Lanzarote are conservative, reserved, predominantly catholic (Protestants are very few and far between on the Canary Islands), and they are well-mannered. They are tolerant towards the tourists and the foreigners living here. Administrative and business affairs are conducted in Castilian (*castellano*), the colloquial language is also Castilian. Influenced by the South American languages, some farmers speak in an almost unintelligible dialect, halves of words are swallowed, and s-sounds left out. In the meantime, an increasing number of Lanzaroteños have learnt to speak German,

English and/or one of the Scandinavian languages. The growing tourism and europisation has meant that the almost timeless life style of the Lanzaroteños has started to change – whose *mañana* (tomorrow) took so many Europeans aback. Daily life has also become busier and more urbane here, differences in social backgrounds are becoming apparent more quickly, encouraging crime and drug addiction; two concepts which were completely unknown before.

Fiesta and Folklore

Fiesta is certainly no strange word for *canarios*. There are more days of celebration on the Canary Isles than in any other place. During the carnivals and bank holidays many people go out and the flights and sea routes are completely booked. The number of religious bank holidays is roughly the same as other European regions, but the holidays for the patron saints of the islands come in addition. On Lanzarote the whole summer comprises a series of fiestas, one following the other.

15. 5 Uga
24. 5 Montaña Blanca
13. 6 Güime
24. 6 Haría
29. 6 Maguez
 7. 7 Femés (San Marcial del Rubicon, patron saint of the island)
16. 7 Teguise; Puerto del Carmen, Tías, Famara, Playa Blanca
24. 8 San Bartolomé
25. 8 Arrecife (San Ginés)
30. 8 Haría (Santa Rosa)
 8. 9 Yaiza (Virgen de los Remedios)
14. 9 Guatiza
15. 9 Mancha Blanca (Tinajo)
30.11 Tao

The main days of the Fiesta are given in the table above. Printed programmes are hung in bars and supermarkets for each fiesta. Villages festivals have a religious and folkloric character, but in most cases they have developed into a sort of fair with motor scooters, shooting galleries and sausage stands. The smaller the village, the more original the fiesta. A fiesta has only one main day, but it begins about two weeks beforehand. The Lanzaroteños enjoy dancing into the night, until six o'clock in the morning. Singers, comedians and show girls perform at the larger celebrations. The fiestas are closed with a show of fireworks (which are sometimes spectacular) and the *asadero*, a communal meal of sardines which the inhabitants of the village and the surroundings participate in. They gather around small fires, sitting on the ground, grilling fish. Traditionally the fish is donated by the fishermen of the village, the wine by the wealthier residents. Today, this part of the fiesta is organised by the mayor's office.

The statutory and religious holidays are different in some cases from those in Europe. Christmas does not have the same value as here (if they have fir trees at all, then they are imported). On the 24. 12, the *canarios* work until evening. They go to Christmas mass, and celebrate Christmas Eve just like New Year and have only one day of celebration at Christmas. New Year is celebrated out on the streets; it is likely and noisy. At midnight it is traditional to eat *uvas de la suerte* (lucky grapes), one for each chime of the clock. The most important feast on the Canary Islands is *Los Reyes*, the Feast of Epiphany. On each island three kings are met at the harbour. They then make their way across the villages in a festival procession, giving presents to hospital patients and the occupants of old people's homes and orphanages. This is the day when Christmas presents are distributed. The Canary carnival is similar to the carnival in Rio de Janeiro. At Easter, *La Semana Santa*, processions make their way through the decorated streets. Corpus Christi is a delightful celebration to see. The streets are decorated with carpets of salt. Because blossom petals are so rare, the Canarians dye sea salt and lay artificially-made carpets of splendid colours showing pictures and ornaments. After the procession, which runs along these carpets, scarcely anything can still be seen of the various motives. The fiestas are the most impressive showcase for Canary folklore. The character of the people is illustrated by their customs, dances and songs. The strong communal spirit amongst the Canarians and their open way is evident. Some of the ancient customs have survived over the years. They tell stories of folk history in songs and dances, accompanied by the guitar, mandoline, lute and *timple*. The *timple* the predominant instrument in folk music, is similar to the ukelele, except its bass string is in the middle. They are made in Teguise. The Canarian songs and melodies sound, in part, oriental. There are performances of folkloric events for tourists. This is one way of maintaining the traditions, which due to modern media, are now fading into the background. Like the island's colours, the costumes are rich in contrast. The peasant woman wears a wide, red ankle-length skirt, with a blue and white striped pinnafore, green blouse and straw hat. Young girls wear a white "tip hat" in addition to the female costume. The peasant dresses in a wide, bright shirt and a black felt hat.

Climate

On the Canary Islands ice cold winters, rainy springs, very hot and dry summers (as in the Mediterranean) and gloomy grey November days are hardly known. The Canary Islands have a climate of "eternal spring", a settled climate, ideal for convalescence. The average precipitation is about one fifth of that of central Europe. Lanzarote and Fuerteventura have an even lower precipitation; in Lanzarote the annual amout is about 135 mm, in Fuerteventura 147 mm. Precipitation is concentrated during the months of November and April. Rainfall is higher on the other islands, due to the higher mountains there. Lanzarote's highest peak measures 670 m, that of Fuerteventura 807 m – too low to touch the rain clouds. Sometimes there is no rainfall all year round, sometimes this lasts for several years.

A maritime climate, a climate influenced by the sea, exists up to a height of 200 m; above 200 m the air becomes fresher and temperatures are more changeable. It is at these heights that the wine is grown, at least in Lanzarote. The temperature changes between 16° and 22° C. The sky is seldom completely free of clouds, July to October is the hottest period, the most pleasant period is between February and July, the most pleasant month of all is May (subject to change). The temperature of the water taken over a whole year is between 18° and 23° C.

The following table is an approximation. One must also consider that different climates can be found of on different islands. On the north and west coasts the temperatures are lower and the precipitation is greater.

Table showing the climate in Lanzarote and Fuerteventura

	Average air temp.	Average water temp.	Humidity (in %)	Days of sun
January	15.3	18	81	18
February	15.7	18	82	16
March	16.2	19	80	20
April	17.2	19	81	18
May	18.1	20	81	18
June	19.6	21	80	16
July	21.5	23	80	13
August	22.4	23	79	12
September	22.1	23	81	17
October	20.7	23	82	18
November	18.5	22	83	17
December	16.3	21	84	16

The Canary Islands are suitable for a sunbathing holiday all year round. Their climate is not only due to their situation in the Atlantic and their proximaty to Africa. While the Sahara, where it is unbearably hot and dry, lies just 100 km east on the same line of latitude, a Mediterranean climate is ensured by the compensatory effect of the wind and water. The middle air temperature are lowered by 2° to 3° compared to those normal on this line of latitude. By the north east trade wind (north of the equator; south of the equator it becomes the south east trade wind) and the cool Canary stream which drifts to the south or south west of the islands. The feeling of heart is appeased by the trade winds. The name trade winds describes those winds on which one can sail to America.

In the region around the equator the sun's rays hit the earth very directly. Warm masses of air rise up, resulting in a relative vacuum on the ground. Cool masses of air stream into this equatorial depression from the north and south; these are diverted slightly by the friction caused by the earth's surface. They then come as the north east (and south east) trade winds. In the morning trade wind clouds form in the mountains at a height of about 600 m before dissolving in the afternoon. The mountains on Lanzarote and Fuerteventura are too low for the formation of trade wind clouds. For this reason these two islands, compared to the others, have a more pronounced continental climate with less precipitation and greater shifts in temperature.

Cool water which has been lifted by the off shore winds rises up on the lee sides resulting in a layer of cold air at a height of more than 100 m. This acts as a barrier against the layers of hot air from the Sahara. However, occasionally it is extremely hot, mainly in the summer months, due to the Sirocco. The temperature can rise by 14°C. The air is full of tiny particles of dust, the horizon has a yellow tinge and the sun is a white disc. The Sirocco has not only brought sand beaches and dunes with it, but also occasionally swarms of migratory locusts (about 10 cm in length), which can devastate the cultivation without end. The last invasion by migratory locusts was in October 1954.

In the winter the trade wind zone, which is dependent on the position of the sun, shifts to the south. The Canary Islands then stand under the influence of rain-bringing atlantic cyclones (a cyclone is an area of low pressure) from the west. These rainfalls, although still rather few and far between, are more than welcomed here in Lanzarote.

Economy

The lack of mineral resources and the barren earth meant that Lanzarote suffered poverty for many years. Agriculture and fishing were the main industries in Lanzarote before tourism developed there. They also bred stock, although less than successfully. Admittedly, the mild climate meant that they were able to cultivate most types of temperature zone crops for most of the year, but the fact that they believed in cultivating one crop only repeatedly brought them into economic difficulties. Onions, corn, wheat, barley, forage plants, fruit, pulses (such as broad beans, lentils and chick peas) are grown for local consumption. The most delicious of the crops grown are the tomatoes, new potatoes and sweet potatoes (also known as batatas). The wine which is pressed here is the best on the Canary Islands (see Cultivation of Unirrigated Land, p.59). Milk, cheese and meat are provided by goats, cow's milk has to be imported. The minimal stock breeding (pigs and game) doesn't even cover the local needs. On the whole agriculture is declining, making up only about 10% of today's gross national product. Domestic food production barely covers 25% of the island's needs. With the development of tourism and the favourable income it brings with it, it looks likely that only subsidiary farming will exist in the future – pursued continuously over a period of time this can do sustained damage to the landscape. Some fields already lie fallow today. The trade balance has been in deficit for some time with imports, particularly from Spain, on the increase. Products from Scandinavia, England and Germany have to be imported for the tourist industry. Apart from construction, on the increase thanks to the tourist boom, industry (25% of the GNP) is restricted to fish canning plants, where tuna is the main fish prepared. Craft objects and embroidery are made by small and cottage industries. Electricity is produced by means of heat technology; some independent suppliers use solar energy plants or wind mills. Tenerife is the site of the second largest refinery in Spain of the C.E.P.S.A. (= *Companía Española de Petróleos, Sociedad Anónima*) oil company; its distilling capacity is 8 million tonnes. 90% of the fuel is produced there. In addition, a power station on Fuerteventura supplies Lanzarote with electrical energy.

The provision of water has always been a problem for the Lanzaroteños. The water balance determined, and still does determine, the quality of life. Small amounts of rain (less than 400 mm in an average year), which are unpredictable both in timing and quantity) trickle through the porous earth or gather in a few places where costly wells (*pozos*) have been installed over impervious layers of rock. After heavier falls of rain the water is pumped from large puddles and water holes into tankers and then into large wells. Collecting tanks can be found on some slopes; they have wells built onto the end of them. In the North, near Mala, a disused dam wall is rotting. Seven *galerías*, natural reservoirs, which are surrounded by layers of impervious rock and which collect rainfall, can be found in the Montañas de Famara. They are opened up by drilling through the rock. Four of the seven *galerías* in the Montañas de Famara have been put into operation. Ten litres of water per second is collected. There is no running ground water on Lanzarote. Previously, in times of emergency, drinking water was transported from Gran Canaria and Tenerife to the island by tanker. Now, with the growing population and the explosion of tourism, more and more water sanitation plants are becoming necessary; using thermal energy sea water is desalinated. Almost all very large urbanisations have a desalination plant today. The tourist centres are the first to be supplied with water, the farmers have to wait their turn. On the Canaries as a whole, three quarters of the agricultural products are irrigated artificially. This is not the case on Lanzarote, where unirrigated cultivation is especially common.

Cultivation of Unirrigated Land

The agricultural cultivation of the Lanzarotean earth was always a hard way to earn a living. A lack of water, the scorching sun and the shriveling winds forced the farmers to be inventive. They use the dry cultivation method, called *secano*, which is characteristic of the Canary archipelago. One form of the dry cultivation method is sand dune culture (*jable*). A section of sand dunes, approximately three to five metres in breadth, runs across the middle of the island between San Bartolomé and Teguise. The sand dunes rise to a maximum height of one metre. If the sand is not deeper than 40 cm, seeds are sowed onto the sand. The roots of the germinating seeds quickly reach the top soil which lies beneath. The sand withholds the moisture and the roots can profit from it. To prevent the dunes from drifting away, the sand is weighed down with stones. They have also recently begun to mix the sand with *picon* (a spanish word). *Picon* is a mixture of volcanic materials, rich in minerals, basaltic lapilli and lava granules, which is very porous and has a hygroscopic effect. *Picon* is a component of a much more frequent method known as *enarenado* (*enarenar* = to sprinkle with sand). This system of dry cultivation was developed by the Canary people themselves. It is known as *enarenado artificial* when the covering layer of volcanic material has to be produced. It is this covering which gives the fields of Lanzarote its typical black colour. The fields are covered in about 10 to 30 cm of *picon*. During the day the volcanic covering heats up, at the same time protecting the top soil from evaporation. The *picon* cools quickly at night, increasing the condensation in the layers of air near to the earth. The *picon* lets the condensation through, and in this way the earth remains continuously moist even without rainfall. The lava granules are changed every ten years. The top layer down to the top soil is removed when seeds are sown. Using a wooden plough which is incapable of making deep furrows, they "scratch" furrows in the ploughland. The plough is drawn by the dromedary. When onions are planted from seeds, contrary to the usual process of sowing, the *picon* is not removed, but furrows are drawn in the covering layer into which the seeds are put.

Lanzarote's wine growing region is situated around La Geria. A wide section of the earth between Uga and San Bartolomé became the natural depository for volcanic material. Here the method of cultivation is known as *enarenado natural*. Deep round funnel-shaped holes have been dug out so that the vines can reach the earth with their roots. This method dates back to the 18th century when the malvasia grape was brought here from Crete. Figs, citrus fruits and almond trees also

grow in La Geria. To protect the vines from the drying wind the wine farmers built walls of volcanic stone around the funnel-shaped holes. The whole area of cultivation covers about 3,000 hectares. One vine is thought to bear up to 50 kg of grapes. The amber coloured malvasia wine, with its spicey, dry bouquet, is the best wine on the Canary archipelago. It thrives on the low rainfall, powerful sun and fertile volcanic earth. For this reason the alcoholic content is very high and even the light wine is as heavy as sherry. It is said to contain the volcanic power, which the Lanzaroteños once feared. The malvasia wine soon became known in Europe and the New World and it is even mentioned in the works of Shakespeare. It was the preferred wine amongst the royal Spanish families and its main customer was England until it was surpassed by sherry, the wines of Bordeaux, madeira and port. In the second half of the 19th century many vines were completed devastated by mildew and the exportation of wine was brought to a standstill. Today the wine is distributed almost exclusively on the Canary archipelago. Different vintages of the ambercoloured malvasia wine can be found in Lanzarote's numerous wine presses along with rose and red wines.

Breeding Dromedaries in Uga

He who observes but casually a dromedary draws the roman plough behind it or how patiently it makes its round of the threshing floor, providing the farmer with invaluable help, cannot deny the animal's dignity. The dromedary, which may at first appear ugly and awkward, is a good natured animal. It is attentive and, apart from in the mating season, gentle and tame. Dromedaries are exemplarary draught and pack animals, they are also good for riding. They are completely at home in the desert, carrying their "larder" on their backs, humps full of fat which keep them going when nothing is available. The dromedary can keep going for up to eight days without food and water and is able to cover a distance of 32 km with a load of 150 kg everyday. Their hard soled hooves and sealable nostrils are adapted to the desert and steppes. They are not only hard, tough workers (their average life expectancy is 35 years), they also provide milk, meat, leather and hair. The dromedary is a ruminant, its dung makes good fuel. It is not entirely clear how dromedaries got to Lanzarote from nearby Africa. It is presumed that García de Herrera brought them with him from his African expeditions. The Lanzaroteños began to breed them. Today they are not so successful. Since 1986 the importation of dromedaries from Morocco has been disallowed due to infectious animal diseases there. Many animals were sold and taken back to Africa. Young dromedaries died repeatedly. The largest breeding ground currently possesses over 200 dromedaries, which live in a large *corral* (a form of paddock) not far from the main road at the edge of Uga. Young dromedaries can be seen from about March there. The female dromedary bears only one child and has to carry the offspring for a term of 12 months. When the young reach two or three it is their turn to be schooled and they are put into use soon after that. Solitary dromedaries are still used to draw the plough, but the majority of these animals from the species of cloven hoofed animals without horns or antlers, carry tourists around in the national park of the Timanfaya. Crouching on their knees, which are protected by thick skin, they wait for customers. They wear muzzles although they do not bite. The rider sits on a green wooden seat on the left and right of the hump. The dromedary gets up with his back legs first, then the front ones – when it sits it is the other way round – and steadily rocks the rider to the top of the mountain. In the afternoon, when their work is done and they have returned to Uga, they are fed in their *corral*. They are given a rest from tourism each year, when they are driven into the steppes, where they stay for several weeks.

Cochineal in Guatiza and Mala

In the north of Lanzarote, near to the east coast, around and in Guatiza and Mala, the visitor may be surprised to see a number of giant cactus fields, the purpose of which is not immediately evident. The fig cactus or opuntia cactus (*opuntia ficus indica*) grows here. It is one of the classic succulent plants which produce delicious fruit and are often for sale. However, that is not the reason why hectares of the opuntia cactus are cultivated. The opuntia was introduced in the 16th century by the Spanish conquistadores, but it was only in the 19th century, when the export of sugar and wine declined, that the Spaniards began to cultivate the beetles on the cactus. The cochineal beetle (*cocus cacti*) which, like the cactus originates from Mexico, feeds parasitically on the flesh of the cactus and is no ordinary beetle. It is responsible for the red carmine acids (*cochineal*), much prized before synthetic dye was developed. It was the farmers of Mexico who first managed an annual production of about 430,000 kg of cochineal, until other countries (India and Africa) also began to breed the beetle. The cochineal beetle arrived on the Canaries in about 1831. It can be recognised by the white down which covers its body. It is fat and round, its body formed in two parts with a conical shaped head. With its

short feelers and thread-like probiscus it guides itself to and feeds parasitically on the flesh of the opuntia cactus. The women farmers are keen to observe that the egg-laying females are evenly distributed on the cacti and that a healthy stream of reproduction can take place. If the weather and climate are good, up to five generations can be bred each year. They are harvested every two to three months. Neither the male of the species, which dies after mating, not the mother beetle are harvested. It is the larva which is scraped from the cactus; it is then killed in hot water and put out to dry in the sun. The dried larva is then made into a powder. In ideal circumstances 300 to 400 kg of beetles can be harvested per hectare per year. Production has declined a great deal since the development of synthetic colour, but for the makers of cosmetics, synthetic dye was not a good replacement. The natural colouring is completely unpoisonous and of the best glowing red. Apart from in the manufacture of lipsticks, cochineal is also used in Persian carpets. Soft drinks, sweets and aperitifs are also coloured with it. 25,000 kg of cochineal is still harvested per year in Lanzarote. About 140,000 insects have to be dried for every kilogramme; for 25 tonnes 3.5 million larva are needed.

Fishing

In the early morning the fishermen draw out of the harbour, in large and small boats, and spend the day at sea. They work between 12 and 16 hours; sometimes they spend the whole day at sea. Even small boats, which are only suited to one day catches, bring large trawls, although fishing is in decline. Fishing takes place from March to October.

The biggest fishing fleet on the Canary archipelago, with 400 ships, is moored in the harbour of Arrecife. This no doubt has to do with the proximity to Africa. The fishing grounds around Africa are especially rich; however, during a fishing war, like that with Morocco in 1983, fishing there can be very dangerous. In this case the fishing fleet stays in Arrecife harbour. The capital is also the site of the fish processing industry. It is mainly tuna fish and sardines which are canned there.

The following are some of the most delicious fish and sea food; *vieja* (spiny loach), *cherne* (stone bass), *sama* (red brace), *salmonete* (red barble), *dorada* (golden brace), *merluza* (hake), *mero* (grouper), *pescadilla* (whiting), *sargo* (a kind of brace), *cabrilla* (goat head fish), *sardina* (sardine), *tiburón* (shark) – there are no dangerous sharks near the coastline – *atún* (tuna), *bonito* (a mackerel-like tuna), *jurél* (a form of mackerel), *lenguado* (sole), *calamar* (squid), *choco* (a kind of squid), *pulp* (octopus), *lapa* (large limpet), *gamba* (shrimps), *langosta* (cray fish) and *cangrej o de mar* (sea crab). (see The Canary Cuisine)

Saltmining or the Salinas of Janubio

Salt, which was once more precious than gold, has waned in importance on Lanzarote. Since fishing has been in decline on the Canary Islands and most fishermen no longer conserve their catch at sea in salt, but in cool boxes, the salt pans have become uneconomical. The last of the great saltpans still in operation lie to the west of Yaiza, by Janubio. Other saltpans have been closed like that on the Costa Teguise in the north in front of the Hotel Las Salinas. Some of them fell victim to the tourist industry, for instance the large plant at Los Pocillos, the Salinas de Matagorda, just a few km east of Puerto del Carmen, where tourist centres stand today.

Janubio is a natural lagoon; sea water is pumped into the man made basins, the *cocederos madres*, which are slightly higher. In previous times it was the windmills standing at the edge of the lagoon which kept the pump mechanism going. The salt water remains in the higher basins for two to four weeks – according to the sun's intensity. It slowly evaporates until it is fed into lower, smaller *cocederos*. It remains here for about another seven days until the salt content has risen to 22°. It is at this point that it is actually fed into the *salinas*. *Salinas* are small basins divided into numerous squares, approximately about two square metres in size. The salt making process comes to and end here. When this sticky mass has crystallised into salt, it is raked together by salt workers for a final drying and piled into small pyramidal heaps.

In earler times 15,000 tonnes of salt was produced per year, now it is only 2,000 tonnes produced under careful management. A small part of the total production is sold as table salt. At the procession for Corpus Christi, the Lanzaroteños dye their domestically produced salt and artfully formed bright carpets with dazzling patterns are laid along the capital's streets and village squares. The majority of the salt is still bought by the fishermen who use it to conserve their catch. The *salina* owners also sell salt water with an increased salt content, the so-called *salmuera*. It has a salt content of 25°. It is prepared in special *cocederos*, transported by tanker and is used in sardine fishing boats for conservation.

When the salt was exported previously, it was put into sacks, transported to Playa Blanca by donkey-led cart and stored in a specially constructed hall. It took a month to load a ship at anchor – it had to rowed across sack by sack. The working conditions in the salt-pans were always very hard. The feet of the barefoot workers were often eaten away. Many workers became blind in old age because their sight had been damaged by the glaring, reflecting light. Nowadays, the owners of the salt pans have great difficulty attracting labour.

Craft and Specialised Craft

The usual type of crafts, which exist here – with some exceptions – like everywhere else, are not the subject of this chapter. Your attention is drawn to some highlights – such as the cobbler in Arrecife, at Calle José Antonio, 41, who still works without machines and delivers solid craft at little cost. Or there is the grain mill at Haría, which, admittedly, is no longer driven by the wind, but by a diesel engine from the turn of the century. Broad belt of leather drive the grinding mechanism. Roast corn, used to make gofio, is ground here along with other grains for local consumption. Haría is also the home of the basket weaver Eulogio. Palm leaf stems are lined up along the wall, obviously out to dry. They are used to make large baskets. He weaves bags, hats and footmats from palm leaves, sometimes using straw and cane as well.

The making of the *timple* is one of the specialised crafts. The *timple* is the five-stringed instrument with its bass string in the middle, which is not dissimilar to the ukelele. It is presumed to originate from the time of the conquerors. The *timple* is an instrument typical of Lanzarote, although it is built on all the islands now. In the former capital of Lanzarote, Teguise, three masters of their trade are still working. One of them taught himself how to make the *timple*. He made his first *timple* at the age of twelve for the fun of it, enjoyed it and refined his from *timple* to *timple*. He can tune the instrument, but not play it. It takes him two days to make the instrument. (You can find him by taking the first street on the left, where the Palacio de Espinola is, from the marketplace in Teguise. His workshop is in the first street to the left). According to the type of wood he uses, it will cost between 6,000 and 15,000 pesetas. In the souvenir shops a *timple* costs between 8,000 and 28,000 pesetas. However, an instruction manual is provided with the latter which shows you how to play the *timple.*

Specialised craft has been partially influenced by European culture since the 15th century; Latin American elements also played a part later. For instance, this is true of embroidery, which is especially popular on La Palma (figurative or patterned embroidery = *bordado*) and Gran Canaria (open embroidery = *calado*). The rosette embroidery (*roseta*) is famous. Working at home, the women embroider little rosettes, which can either be used as place mats or can be sewed together as covers and table cloths.

Ceramics are a vestige of the old Canary culture. Using techniques handed down over the years, ceramicists are still making vessels without a potting wheel. They smoothe out the tone with stones and bake the ceramics in a sort of bread oven or in the open fire. These "fire ceramics" are perfect imitations of the ceramics of the ancient

Canary people. A small house stands on the roof of the Castillo San Gabriel, the Museum of Archeology. This is the show case for the pots, jugs and archaic figures by Juan Brito, the curator of the museum. Brito has made a name for himself as ceramicist and sculptor. Doña Dorothea, who is more than 90 years old, pots away near to Munique (between Tiagua and Soo). Her family has been making pottery for many generations. You can find her work in several shops, but can also buy directly from her: in Muñique, first street on the left. Dorothea's house is about 2 km along on the right hand side.

Art and Culture

Apart from natural features and the sights, most of which have been built by the artist and sculptor César Manrique (see The New Architecture or Manrique, p. 73; and Places – Sights – Beaches, p. 80), the cultural landscape is rather bare. Arrecife is the main place where exhibitions are mounted, in the Almacén, for instance, where the cellar of an old well was made into the *El Aljibe* gallery. The mayor's office in Yaiza opened up an arts centre (*Casa de la cultura*). Almost next door a private gallery has been opened by a German which is worth visiting. A changing programme of exhibitions is shown there (paintings and ceramics are sold), accommodating works of unknown painters and sculptors along with Aquilars and César Manriques.

Nor are there many concerts apart from the performances of folklore. Concerts are sometimes put on in the Cueva de los Verdes, in the concert room of Los Jameos del Agua or in the San José Museum in Arrecife. In 1968 Manrique incorporated an interesting museum for contemporary art into the Castillo San José. The collection also includes artists from far away from the islands. The Castillo de San Gabriel in Arrecife houses an archeological museum. The curator of it is the self taught Juan Brito, who was born in 1919 in the north of Lanzarote. Like the original inhabitants, he makes pots and jugs without throwing them; his archaic figures tell the tales of ancient Canary history. His works are exhibited in a little house on the roof of the Castillo. Ildefonso Aquilar is one of the island's best known artists. Aquilar, a painter, composer and photographer was born in Salamanca in 1945, but has lived on the island since 1946. He paints landscapes with acrylic resins and volcanic ash. He composes electronic and meditative music, using natural sounds and by sometimes playing around with them. He uses his compositions as sound tracks to audio visual works, one of the best known being "Erosion". With a succession of slides he puts photographic films together and plays with natural forces. According to his statements, he symbolizes the seventh day of Creation – which is still to come on the island. Aquilar is one of César Manrique's followers.

The New Architecture or César Manrique

"The Canary architecture is a modest form of Andalusian baroque and it is at its most modest on Lanzarote where poverty was greater than on Tenerife and Gran Canaria. However, this also makes its forms the purest" (César Manrique).

The island in its present form is unthinkable without César Manrique. His influence and work have left their mark on the island's face. The Lanzaroteños credit him with "having made Lanzarote". Manrique was a painter, sculptor, architect (without having studied), ecologist, curator of monuments, town planner, garden- and landscape architect; César Manrique was the most outstanding artistic personality on Lanzarote, in fact on the whole archipelago. This vivacious, unconventional and friendly man was born on 24 April 1919 in Arrecife. He volunteered to fight on Franco's side in the Spanish Civil War. When he returned to Lanzarote his first successful exhibitions took place. In 1945 he moved to Madrid, where he began to study at La Escuela de Bellas Artes, funded by a scholarship. In 1950 he graduated in fine art and art education. Shortly afterwards he enrolled at the film school, which he quickly left. In La Era, a garden restaurant in Yaiza, the last evidence of his Madrid school paintings can be seen, three figurative paintings using faience which depict fishing, agriculture and winegrowing. In 1953 Manrique began to paint abstract compositions (a virtual revolt in Franco's Spain) and exhibited a year later with his friends Manuel Manpaso and Luis Féito who shared the same ideas. Manrique went his own way without following

a certain school, avoiding overinfluence by his mentors Pablo Picasso and Henri Matisse. By the end of the '50s Manrique had made a name for himself in Madrid. Exhibitions followed in the capitals of Europe, Japan and the USA which led to international repute. He received prizes and was selected for the first time for the Venice Biennale; four years later he was re-selected. In 1963 his girlfriend and life companion, with whom he had spent 18 years, died. This painful experience was probably the impetus behind his move to New York two years later, where he had been offered a post at the International Institute for Art Education. A few weeks after his arrival he was taken on by the gallerist Catherine Viviano. Suddenly César Manrique was hanging alongside his famous co-patriot Joan Miró and next to Max Beckmann. In 1968 Manrique travelled directly from New York to Lanzarote, which he found much as he had left it. He had the feeling that the island needed him. He made himself into its advocate and was made its advocate. The fact that many of Manrique's ideas were realized owes much to his indefatiguable energy, his persistence, his expertise and not least the degree of international celebrity he enjoys. He propagated a form of elite tourism, felt "bound" to help the poverty stricken island where the population was supposed to be evacuated 50 years before. Manrique dreamed of "a paradise for the few who have an eye for the special". His dream failed. But he skillfully carried through his building plans with his old friend José Ramírez Cerdá, president of the Cabildo Insular at that time. Luis Morales, who also worked at the Cabildo, provided Manrique with a congenial partner.

Working as a site foreman, he understood how to put Manrique's ideas into practice. Manrique never drew any plans. He designed the buildings and details on the spot, mostly orally, sometimes he made a sketch on a serviette or made a chalk drawing of the ground plan on the earth. This was the case with the restaurant building at the Castillo San José. For Manrique the key lies in the open country. He had to draft plans, abandon them or correct them on the very site, not in the studio. This was a daring process. Manrique did not need the security of a plan, he exposed himself to an open creative process, which can fail at any time. Building plans were often only signed and approved afterwards long after the last handshake had already been made. These are just a few of his buildings: the Castillo San José in Arrecife, the Fertility Monument in the geographical centre of the island, Mirador del Río on the steep north bank, the airport at Arrecife, Los Jameos del Agua on the north east coast, the Hotel Las Salinas and a complete settlement: Pueblo Marinero on the Costa Teguise, or the El Diablo restaurant on the Islote del Hilario in the Fire Mountains, the Jardín de Cactus in Guatiza and the Fundación César Manrique in Tahiche. (In addition, there is a whole series of sights, which are literally worth seeing. These are discussed in more detail in the capital Places-Sights-Beaches, p. 80.) Manrique shaped the architectural policy and his influence can be seen everywhere on the island. He was able to persuade the authorities to inflict a complete ban on advertising hoardings and was made artistic director of the construction company, Rio Tinto, which owns a large part of the north of the island. He was also able to persuade his fellow directors to run telephone and power lines underground. Up to now only one sky scraper has been built, the Gran Hotel in Arrecife, which Manrique describes as "a crime against the spirit of the island". Manrique is said to have been in New York for some time when it was being built. He promoted a traditional cubic architectural form. A house can grow; the Lanzaroteños begin with one or two rooms, when the family grows, they build new one- or two storey cubes onto it. The rooms surround a patio which incorporates a well. Manrique's notion was to build in accordance with nature and to help extend natural forms. His aim was to preserve tradition and to realize a form of architecture which was suited to the landscape and which was suited in particular to the island's natural features. He was in direct contact with nature, working from and with it. He was also a person who was aware of his fellow beings and considers them in his work. He has brought nature out from behind the scenes, made it visible, preventing overdevelopment by supporting the construction of tourist centres. He designed a form of architecture which was conducive to a pleasant life style. Manrique proposed the projects, planned them, saw them through, but took no

commission. His work was a present to the people of Lanzarote. Manrique lived from his private commissions and his painting. He realized his desire to live with the lava in his own house in Tahiche, which he has recently endowed to his fellow citizen. He erected the house, with its characteristic, Lanzarotean cubic form, across seven volcanic bubbles on a bluish black lava stream. Apart from the bell tower, the external architectural form of the house is not much different from the other houses (→ Fundación César Manrique). He has made a house of the Muses out of the lava bubbles, hollow chambers about five metres in diameter, which were formed as the lava solidified. Manrique took care of nature avoiding ugly architectural forms. And it was his aim to protect Lanzarote from bad construction. He has, in part, succeeded. He has also made the architecture more uniform. The whitewashed walls, doors and windows painted green and the almost uniform cubic architectural style recur so often that it becomes almost unbearable. A red tiled roof, a beige external wall, or a door or window turning slightly blue are refreshing sights. But these are mere details, compared to his great achievements. Manrique was the impetus behind a humane form of architecture, he set decisive accents. However, his influence was not enough, capitalist interests were pushed through; ever more barbarians were at work. The

architectural style which was developed from the traditional style was being imitated and turned into kitsch.

Manrique himself spoke of "stupid, brutal speculators". After the firm of Río Tinto – where Manrique was once artistic director – experienced economic difficulties, commercial interests grew. Market forces became the decisive factor behind new construction and the firm built indiscriminately, no longer heeding the artist's advice. They built with complete disregard for the many agreements made for many years; indeed they are still building. Manrique's name was also misused for their own purposes, although he had long since resigned from Río Tinto. He died at the age of seventy-three years, fit and full of vitality in a tragic accident near Arrecife on 25th September 1992 six months after the opening of his foundation, which he left during his lifetime to the population of Lanzarote.

Places – Sights – Beaches

This chapter lists places, sights and beaches in alphabetical order. Travel agencies offer various bus tours around the north and south of the island, a crater tour in the Timanfaya national park, an evening of folklore in Uga or a night in Jameos del Agua. You can take part in jeep or photo safaris, fly to Morocco or visit other islands. It is best to get information on what trips are available when you are at the travel agents. There are no details of round islands trips here, this chapter is meant as a guide to discovering the island yourself (by renting a car, for instance). However, below two worthwhile tours are outlined (using only the names of places). Both have Puerto del Carmen, the most popular tourist spot, as their starting point.

North tour
Puerto del Carmen – Tías – San Bartolomé – Al Campesino (the Fertility Monument) – La Caleta – Teguise (optional trip to the Castillo Santa Bárbara) – Los Valles – Haría – Mirador del Río – Yé – Cueva de los Verdes – Jameos del Agua (optional trip to Orzola) – Punta de Mujeres – Arrieta – Mala – Guatiza (optional trip to the Costa Teguise) – Tahiche – Arrecife – Puerto del Carmen (about 156 km including optional trips).

South tour
Puerto del Carmen – Mácher (optional trip to Playa Quemada) – Femés – (on temporary road) Playa Blanca – (on temporary road) the beaches of Papagayo – Playa Blanca – Salinas de Janubio – Los Hervideros – El Golfo – (on temporary road) Yaiza – Montañas del Fuego – Mancha Blanca – Tinajo (optional trip to La Santa) – Tiagua – Tao – Mozaga – Al Campesino (the Fertility Monument) – Masdache – La Geria – Uga – Mácher – Puerto del Carmen (about 157 km including optional trips).

These tours outlined above are suggestions for routes to follow. They are certainly rather strenuous if carried out in one day only.

Places

Arrecife   The capital and administrative centre of Lanzarote is the home of 30,000 people. Translated, Arrecife means rocky reef. In the town's harbour stands the largest fishing fleet of the Canary archipelago. The townscape of white cubic houses was spoilt by some hotels, most notably by the Arrecife Gran Hotel with its fifteen storeys. It is the only high rise building on the island. Banks, shops, bars and restaurants can be found on the sea promenade, the Avenida del Generalissimo Franco and in the Calle León y Castillo, which runs from the Castillo de San Gabriel (see there) into town. The nearby parallel streets also have many shops and bars. Going towards the Charco de San Ginés, the small lake, which was formed and delicately reinforced and bridged by Manrique, one comes across the simple church Parroquia San Ginés with its square tower and colonial facade. Continuing in this direction one reaches the harbour and the Castillo de San José (see there). Arrecife is a town to discover oneself. The town does not have so very much to offer, but there are nice corners, cosy bars and little bodegas, popular meeting places where you can have a drink with the natives and study the islanders. The Almacén (see there) in Calle José Betancort, 33 is recommended. Typical specialities of this café are *churros* (Viennese whirls) and a glass of hot cocoa. In addition, the restaurant in the Castillo San José by the harbour and the Chinese restaurant Taiwan in Calle Canalejas are recommended (see the map of the town on the back cover). The main day of the fiesta is 25 August.

Arrieta   This village on the north coast should not be left out when a tour of the north is made. Not just because of the nearby sights such as Los Jameos del Agua and the Cueva de los Verdes. The north tour can be ended here with a first class meal of fish. The El Ancla restaurant and the Restaurante Miguel at the harbour mole are both good and one can eat there at reasonable prices with a wonderful view of the mole and sea. Petrol station.

La Caleta   A small fishing village, 16 km from Mozaga and 8 km north of Teguise. This is home to one of the most beautiful beaches in Lanzarote, the Playa de Famara. In contrast to others, this beach has a rough sea climate. The current is dangerous, the coast suitable for surfing and wave riding. It is worth taking a walk through the actual village, where a number of bars and restaurants can be found.

Costa Teguise   is the third largest tourist centre in Lanzarote after Puerto del Carmen (see there) and Playa Blanca (see there). In 1977 the foundation stone for this area was laid with the construction of the five star hotel "Los Salinas" (worth-seeing), which César Manrique helped to design. Further hotels, apartments, shops, bars and restaurants were built in quick succession. The well-kept 18 hole golf course is international standard.

Femés   This mountain village can be reached from Uga by crossing Las Casitas. It is situated in a wind gap, which provides a wonderful vantage point over Montaña Roja and Playa Blanca. At the start of the village there is a small restaurant offering good young goat and a sun terrace. The church was officially opened on 17th February 1733, during the mighty volcanic eruptions (1730–1736). It carries the name of the island's patron saint: Marcial del Rubicon. This is also the name of the fiesta, which has its main day on the 7th July.

La Geria   The island's wine growing area is a large man-made landscape. A separate crater for each malvasia vine is dug out and a small protecting wall is built on the upper edge. With laborious, detailed work wine is cultivated up to the very top of the volcano, producing a strange form of landscape architecture. (see Cultivation of Unirrigated Land, p. 59)

Arrecife

El Golfo   For one part El Golfo is a crater, half engulfed by sea, its crescent soaring upwards, before a black beach and green lagoon, fed underground by the sea. For the other part El Golfo is a village. Turning west at the Salinas of Janubio, passing Los Hervideros (see there), one follows the road through Lanzarote's bizarrest landscape, closely following the west coast, about 8 km until the street ends in a park square. A short footpath to the lagoon, which is rich in micro-organisms, begins here. Because of frequent thefts you are advised not to leave any valuable items in the car. You can reach the village by taking the turning on the right of the park square and travel around the *Montaña del Golfo*. The houses are used most at the week ends; El Golfo is a holiday spot for the natives. It is also becoming a good place for fish restaurants; there are already seven of them there now.

Guatiza   Like Mala the village borders on the cactus plantations where the cochineal beetle is bred. An interesting windmill can be seen between Guatiza and Mala, around which Manrique planted a cactus garden in the middle of the cactus plantation (see Cochineal in Guatiza and Mala; and Jardín de Cactus). The main day of the fiesta: 14 September.

Haría   Situated in the valley of a thousand palms, this village has an oriental feel to it. Or Moorish. The North African architecture, the cubic white houses and the numerous palm trees give this impression. The palm which has taken to this place most is the golden fruit palm; its fruit is not edible however. Haría often gives the impression of being a ghost town, although almost 3,000 people live there. If one approaches Teguise from Los Valles, there is a wonderful view of the village from the pass road at the Mirador del Haría, a small souvenir shop. In the centre of the village one can enjoy the shadow and peace under the Benjamin trees and acacias. There are several bars and restaurants where one can eat and drink. Chemist. Main day of the fiesta: 30 August.

Mácher   Situated between Uga and Tías. Village passed on the way to elsewhere. Turning for Puerto del Carmen and, by crossing La Asomada, to the wine growing region. Petrol station.

Mala   The village is situated in the north east of the island between Guatiza and Arrieta and is surrounded by cactus plantations, where the cochineal beetle is bred. (see Cochineal in Guatiza and Mala, p. 64)

El Golfo

Haría

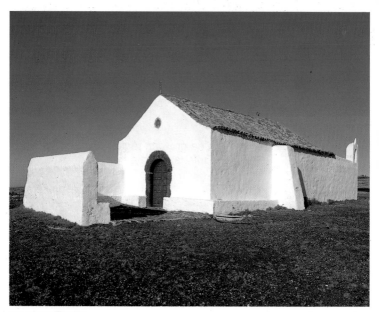

Ermita de Teguise

Playa Blanca

Mancha Blanca   Situated between the Montañas del Fuego and Tinajo, the area was the victim of the last volcanic eruptions in 1824. The Ermita de los Dolores is worth seeing. The church dates from the 18th century and is the home of the volcanic saint: Nuestra Señora de los Volcanes. According to legend Dolores diverted the burning stream of lava, flowing from Volcano Quemada, with her hand and saved the farmers' houses and fields from obliteration. Main day of the fiesta: 15 September.

Masdache   Situated in the wine growing region between La Geria and Mozaga. The bodega El Grifo is worth a mention.

Mozaga   The Fertililty Monument stands here (see there) in the geographical centre of Lanzarote.

Muñique   Unspectacular as a village, but the house of the cera-micist Doña Dolores can be found on the temporary street from Muñique to El Cuchillo. One can buy archaic figures and handmade pottery from here. Muñique is situated between Tiagua and Soo.

Orzola   The name probably originates from "oursolle", the old de-scription for orchilla, the lichen used for dye. Orzola, the most northerly village in Lanzarote, 9 km from Los Jameos del Agua, is a dreamy place which is well worth visiting. From here you can take a long boat to Graciosa (departure 10.00, return about 17.00) or travel to Montaña Clara and Alegrenza with the fishermen. There are beautiful beaches, covered in a fine layer of Muschelkalk on the way to Orzola from Jameos del Agua. The Playa de la Cantería (see there) is to the west of Orzola. It is dangerous to swim at the end of the cove in Orzola, the current is very strong and it even causes larger boats trouble. Fresh fish and sea food are proffered in several restaurants.

Playa Blanca   This former sleepy fishing village is gradually be-coming a second Puerto del Carmen. Buildings are merrily going up in the region of the Papagayo beaches and, in the other direction, towards the lighthouse, Faro de Pechiguera. One can sit and look across to Fuerteventura at the many bars and restaurants along the delightful beach promenade. The beach itself is small and usually crowded. Trips are offered five times a day from the harbour, where fishing boats are moored alongside yachts, to Corralejo on Fuerte-ventura by ferry (departure from Playa Blanca to Corralejo: 8.00, 10.00, 14.00, 16.00, 18.00. Return from Corralejo to Playa Blanca: 9.00, 11.00, 15.00, 17.00, 19.00). Petrol station. Main day of the fiesta: 16 July.

Playa Quemada   Playa Quemada is still an authentic village with it's own black beach, which will be developed turistically in the future.

Puerto del Carmen   The main tourist spot on Lanzarote. Two thirds of all holiday makers come here. A sand beach, about 12 km in length stretches between the old part of this erstwhile fishing village and the airport. This international holiday centre correspondingly stretches from Playa Blanca across Playa de los Pocillos to Matagorda. There is lots to do. During the day the glorious beaches invite sunbathers; surfers, divers and anglers will find plenty of others pursuing these interests. Although the beaches are very popular, it is possible to find a quiet spot. The coastal road which separates the tourist centres from the beach carries heavy traffic. Apartment and bungalow blocks make up the greater part of the accommodation, but in the Hotel San Antonio and Hotel Los Fariones well kept, high class accommodation can be found. Judging by the many supermarkets, there are many self-catering holiday makers here. There is an abundance of shops, bars and restaurants (see Special Restaurants).

There are a number of restaurants which, having once specialised in Canary dishes, now offer an array of international dishes. There is no lack of entertainment (see Brief Survey of Puerto del Carmen). Chemist, petrol station. Main day of the fiesta: 16 July.

Punta de Mujeres Situated between Jameos del Agua and Arrieta, it is a small fishing hamlet, which is still idyllic today.

San Bartolomé The village is situated in what is almost the geographical centre of the island and forms a traffic junction. It is the centre of agriculture. 4,700 people live here. San Bartolomé is also the home of Lanzarote's best known folklore group. There is a public library here and a beautifully laid out village square with the church of Parroquia de San Bartolomé at one end. There is a petrol station between San Bartolomé and the Monumento al Campesino. Main day of the fiesta: 24 August.

La Santa The sports centre of the same name is situated after the fishing village of La Santa, 8 km north east on Tinajo. It is the largest sports centre in Europe.

Tahiche Situated about 6 km north of Arrecife, the village is interesting for several reasons. For one thing, the former dwelling-house of César Manrique, which is now a museum and foundation, is situated here on the San Bartolomé road. For another, this is the starting point to the route to the Restaurante Los Aljibes, worth visiting for its architecture. Manrique integrated the restaurant into some former wells. If you are coming from Arrecife, you can reach it by turning right at the crossing where the left hand road is marked to San Bartolomé. Turning right, you go under a gate, also made by Manrique, in the direction of Costa Teguise. The renovated wells are situated about 100 m further on the right. By driving about 1 km further, you reach the golf course of the Costa Teguise.

Tao Village in the centre of the island, between Tiagua and Mozaga (Monumento al Campesino, see there). Main day of the fiesta: 30 November.

Teguise   Teguise, Lanzarote's most beautiful town stands beneath the Guanapays (452 m), on which the Genoan Lanzarotto Malocello had the Castillo de Guanapay (also called Santa Bárbara) built in the 14th century. Teguise was once the island's capital and a diocesan town. Maciot de Béthencourt had founded the town in the 15th century and had it laid out in its chess-board formation. It has a Mexican feeling about it, which can be attributed to the houses built in the Spanish colonial style. The interesting wooden doors and windows are rich in carving, some of the balconies are typical of the Canaries; each one has a different kind of ornamentation. The town is situated a little distance from the sea due to the numerous pirate attacks. From here one can see far into the land in an easterly direction, but Teguise was protected in the north by the precipitous coast. Nevertheless, the *Callejón de la Sangre* (the lane of blood) is a memorial to the attack by the pirate Morato Arráez in 1586 which ended in a bloody massacre. The market place is surrounded by Teguise's most beautiful buildings: the church of Parroquia San Miguel (1680), which has a famous madonna figure; the Palacio de Espinola, named after the Genoan merchant Vicente Spinola, today it is a museum well worth visiting. The Acatife stands opposite the church of San Miguel; it is a bodega and restaurant offering good food. A typical town house stands next to it; today it is the home of a decorative arts shop, where you can buy embroidery, fire ceramics and all sorts of objets d'art. Two monasteries make up the townscape – the Franciscan monastery of San Francisco

de Miraflores, built in the 16th century and the Santa Domingo monastery, built in the 18th century. This century also saw the birth of the writer José Clavijo y Fajarde, probably Teguise's best known citizen. Clavijo was director of theatre at the court of Carlos III of Spain. In Madrid he seduced the milliner Lisette Caron, the sister of Pierre Augustin Caron de Beaumarchais, who was at that time living in Paris. Beaumarchais endeavoured to blackmail Clavijo into promising marriage to his not-so young sister; sadly his attempts were in vain. Beaumarchais eternalised the episode in his play "Eugénie". Goethe made use of the material as a model for his tragedy "Clavigo".

Teguise is also famous for its *timple*, which is made here and is amongst one of the most frequently played string instruments on the Canary archipelago. It was invented in the 19th century by Mr John Timple. It is rather like the ukelele, the most important difference being that the *timple's* bass string is in the middle. You can find *timple* of varying quality (see: Craft and Specialised Crafts, p. 70). A market is held in Teguise on Sundays. Folklore groups sometimes perform. Artists sell pictures. There is also jewellery and ceramics for sale. Gypsies sell embroidery. The Lanzaroteños offer goat's cheese, fruit, vegetables and fish for sale. There are snack stalls, selling drinks and delicious bites to eat. A trip to the Castillo de Guanapay (see there) is certainly worthwhile; one can see over Teguise and large parts of the island. Chemist. Main day of the fiesta: 16 July. Teguise is probably the most delightful village in Lanzarote.

Tiagua   Only of significance as a point of orientation and a place passed enroute. You can travel to Muñique (see there) from here.

Tías   Situated in the south east on the main road between Mácher and Arrecife. It is the site of an interesting church, the Parroquia de Nuestra Señora de la Candelaría, which can be viewed during mass (*santa misa*). For self caterers it is cheaper to shop here (and in Arrecife) than in the main tourist centres. The butcher's (*carnicería*) is recommended. Chemist. Petrol station. Ambulance. Main day of the fiesta: 16 July.

Tinajo   Capital of the district of the same name, which also encompasses the Timanfaya national park. Has about 3,000 inhabitants and is situated between Mancha Blanca and La Santa. The church bears a sun dial from the year 1881. Petrol station. Chemist.

Uga   This sleepy, African looking spot is situated on the edge of the volcanic landscape between Mácher and Yaiza. Dromedaries are bred here (see Breeding Dromedaries in Uga, p. 62). Uga has an exotic air, especially in the early afternoon when the dromedaries return from work and are herded along the streets. Uga is the home of the most famous school (along with Telde on Gran Canaria) of *Lucha canaria*, Canary wrestling. There is good service in the Bar Casa Gregorio. The *cabrito frito* is particularly delicious.

Los Valles   The valleys. They are situated 5 km from Teguise on the way to Haría. Interesting landscape. The terraced fields are impressive as is the view towards the south when one reaches the end of the valley.

Yaiza   The village is situated to the west of Arrecife between Uga and the Salinas de Janubio and is home to about 2,000 inhabitants. With its white houses punctuated solitary palms, Yaiza is the most impressive village in Lanzarote (along with Haría). It has already been considered twice in the annual election of Spain's most beautiful village. Yaiza has an African feeling about it. The facades of some of the houses show that the more affluent islanders live here. Looking to the north, one's glance falls on the Timanfaya national park and the Fire Mountains. The parish church Nuestra Señora de los Remedios dates from the 18th century. The main day of the fiesta is the 8th September. It is one of the most beautiful feasts on the island. The bar on the road leading through is authentic. In the El Volcan restaurant next door, it is worth sampling the *puchero*, a Canary casserole of meat and vegetables, assuming that hundreds of tourists are not being served at the same

time. The garden restaurant La Era is particularly delightful; it has a very pleasant ambience. Chemist. Petrol station. The Yaiza gallery is worth a visit. One can buy pictures and pottery there; various exhibitions are held. Open from 17.00–19.00. In the fortress, an emigrant museum has been erected.

Yé Not important as a village. Situated in the north between Maguez and Mirador del Río (see there). The landscape is worth seeing.

Sights

Almacén Is situated in Arrecife (see there) in the Calle José Betancort, 33, and was once a residential house (*almacén* = store, department store). Manrique and others bought it and opened it as a arts centre in 1974. It was of course Manrique who was in charge of the conversion. Today the Almacén is owned by the municipality. There is a bar, the Pablo Ruiz Picasso restaurant, a book store and a furniture and design shop. In the cellar Manrique had an old well turned into the El Aljibe gallery. Opposite the Almacén are the artist's former offices, which now form a small museum.

Castillo de las Coloradas Stands on the Punta del Aquila one km east of Playa Blanca (see above) and dates from the 18th century. From here one can gain a wonderful view right across the sea. This is the point from which "attackers" were once spotted. One can see across the Papagayo beaches to Playa Blanca and across to the next island, Fuerteventura. The Castillo itself is locked.

Castillo de Guanapay Also called Castillo Santa Bárbara. Lanzarotto Malocello built the Castillo towards the end of the 14th century. In 1596 it was converted and reinforced by the fortress architect Leonardo Torriani. Spain's high society withdrew to the Castillo in times of war. From Guanapay one has a glorious view of Teguise and the surrounding countryside.

Castillo de Guanapay

Castillo de San Gabriel Situated on the Isla de San Gabriel near Arrecife (see there), the Castillo was originally a wooden fortress, which could not withhold the many attacks by pirates. It was reinforced twice. The first time was in 1572 by the Spanish fortress builder Sancho de Selín, who turned the Castillo into a stone fort. The second time was according to the plans of Leonardo Torriani. It was reinforced in 1590, after the reinforcements of 1586 proved too flimsy, to withhold a pirate attack by Morato Arráez. Today the Castillo houses an archeological museum. You can reach the Castillo from the sea promenade across a stone dam or a rail bridge, the *Puente de las Bolas* (the ball bridge), which is the emblem of Lanzarote. Open from Monday to Friday 9.00–14.45.

Castillo de San José   The fortress was built between 1776–1779, no longer to secure the harbour de Naos for the military; there was nothing left to defend. With the construction of the Castillo, King Carlos III rather aimed to appease the lack of food. The Lanzaroteños suffered from lack of food continuously between 1703 and 1779. It was for this reason that the Spanish king tried to provide work with the *Fortaleza del Hambre* (Hunger fortress) and to make survival easier. Claudio de Lisle had the fortress built 70 m above the harbour of Arrecife. Until 1890 the fortress was used as a powder store, afterwards it stood empty. In 1968 César Manrique suggested renovating the Castillo and fitting it out as a museum for contemporary art (Museo de Arte Contemporáneo). An institution was founded and Manrique was made its honorary director. It was also he who took charge of the architecture and put the collection together. It was

Castillo de San José

opened in 1976 with big names: Joan Miró, Pablo Picasso, Sam Francis, Antonio Tápies and many others. Manrique put together a museum which matched up to the standards of the world wide art scene. The paintings and sculpture are changed regularly. The collection cost the citizens of Lanzarote not one peseta. At the Castillo Manrique also had a restaurant built, the ground plans of which he drew directly onto the earth with chalk – without any draft. Today one can dine there looking down at the harbour and with pleasant music playing in the background. It is even played in the toilets. Concerts are occasionally given in the upper exhibition hall. The Castillo is open from 11.00–21.00, the restaurant from 11.00–24.00, you can dine from 13.00–15.30 and after 20.00 (see Arrecife).

Cueva de los Verdes   It is situated in the north of Lanzarote, south east of the Monte Corona. The Cueva de los Verdes (Green Cave) is part of a 7 km long underground system and, along with Los Jameos del Agua (see there) it is one of the most interesting volcanic manifestations on the island. The tunnel-like caves were created by a pre-historic eruption of Volcano Corona. A broad stream of lava swirled towards the east coast, but it first cooled quickly on the surface and became hard. Underneath, the lava that was still hot streamed on. By melting away old basaltic rocks, the lava eroded and flowed out. Hollow chambers were able to form. Several galleries lie above each other. In the 17th century the Lanzaroteños used these galleries to hide from slave traders and pirates. A path around the caves and corridors, which is about 2 km long has been made for tourists. Jesús Soto provided a form of lighting which has a theatrical effect. A corresponding, often sacral sort of music is played to complete the atmosphere; it seems to emerge from every stone. The acoustics are marvelous. The cave walls, with their lava drip stone or "stone drawings" sometimes give the impression of drawings or paintings. One corridor becomes a hall which is actually used for concert performances and can hold 1,000 visitors. At the end of the round trip: a profound hole. Or so it seems. But find out for yourself. From the south you reach the Cueva de los Verdes via Arrieta or via Haría and Yé. Los Jameos del Agua are only two kilometres away; they belong to the same system of caves. The Cueva de los Verdes is open from 10.00–17.00, it costs 600 pesetas per person. There are tours on the hour and every half hour.

Fundación César Manrique   In his unpublished New York diary, César Manrique wrote in 1966 of his homesickness for Lanzarote. At the time he was still undecided as to where to set up his permanent studio. His desire to live with the lava was put into action two years later in his own house which he had built in Taro de Tahíche, and which he lived in until 1987. He donated it to his fellow citizens as a foundation in 1992. Above five volcanic bubbles, on a blue-black lava flow, he built an architectural masterpiece in Lanzarotean cubic form. He cleverly integrated the caverns into the basic outline of the living area of 1500 square metres. The cellar-deep volcanic bubbles, connected by tunnels, became temples to the muse, each in its own different colour. This palazzo is an impressive example of Manrique's idea of landscape-related architecture. A fig-tree which had already taken root previously grows up from the red volcanic bubble into the living-room above, now an exhibition room in which Manrique's private collection is displayed. On show are works by Manrique: oil paintings, drawings, sketches, sculptures, ceramics, photographs and plans

both of works actually carried out and works never produced. For Manrique, who was seventy-three at the inauguration in March 1992, it was a dream come true. He regarded the foundation as the reward of his life's work: "The Foundation is my personal testament which I bequeath to the people of Lanzarote, and which I hope will serve to keep alive the promotion of art, the integration of architecture into nature, the environment, and preserve the cultural and natural values of our island." The Fundación César Manrique is open from Monday to Friday 10.00–19.00 and Saturday and Sunday from 10.00–14.00. There is integrated a café and a book-shop.

Los Hervideros   Situated in the middle between the Salinas of Janubio (see there) and El Golfo (see above). Los Hervideros is a "volcanic exhaust pipe", which leads to the sea. The erosions in the cliff are interesting and fountains of water when the seas are high.

Los Jameos del Agua   The Los Jameos del Agua, 250 m from the north east coast, were created, like Cueva de los Verdes (see above) during a prehistoric eruption of the Monte Corona. It is part of the same system of caves and cavities which has a series of cave entrances and broken cave roofs. If one climbs down into the first "bubble", which is open at the top, the artificially laid tropical flora is at once impressive. This is immediately recognisable as the work of César Manrique. A natural lagoon, a saltwater lake, which is connected to the sea underground, gave the grotto its name. A hole in the cave roof, which was presumably caused by a gas explosion – the stopper lies intact on the ceiling of the cave very close by – allows rays of sun through, which make the lake shimmer a dark turquoise, sometimes bluish black, sometimes steel blue. Little white, blind crabs live on the ground. These are rare shellfish, about 3 cm in length, albino crabs (*Munidopsis polimorpha*), designed to live deep in the sea, about 1,000 metres down. No certain explanation has been given for its appearance in Los Jameos del Agua. Jesús Soto and Luis Morales, both experienced architects, put César Manrique's ideas into practice. It was due to their collaboration with Manrique that a restaurant, night club, small bars and a concert cave were created. They all show a wonderful flair for architecture and have marvelous acoustics. Concerts and ballet are occasionally staged here. Unfortunately, it is very difficult to discover the dates, since no programmes are produced, but it is well worth asking around a little and experiencing a performance in the concert cave. If one follows the zig zag staircase up, one comes to a kind of walk along the battlements, which leads along the edges of the caves. At this point there is also a row of flat buildings which are destined to become a Parador Nacional. (Paradores Nacionales are hotels run by the Ministry for Tourism). A museum for volcaneology has been created. Los Jameos del Agua is open daily from 11.00–18.45, it costs 700 ptas. On Tuesday, Friday and Saturday it is open from 19.00–03.00 in addition, when there is dancing. It costs 1000 ptas. Access is via Arrieta or from the Cueva de los Verdes.

Jardín de Cactus   César Manrique even erected a monument to cactus. Around and at Guatiza and Mala, in the north of the island, the visitor is surprised by the gigantic cactus fields used for the cultivation of cochineal. Like the fig cactus (opuntia ficus indica), the cochineal louse (coccus cacti) has been imported from Mexico. The cochineal louse is a parasite on the fleshy lobes of the opuntia, but its larvae supply the red dye of carmine acid, which was once greatly coveted, before the invention of aniline dyes. Right in the middle of this agricultural landscape, at the foot of the mill of Guatiza, the government has had a cactus garden laid out according to Manrique's ideas. In front of it is an eight-metre metal cactus statue, loosely based on the cactus pachycereus grandis. Turning this eroded place with its bizarrely weathered monoliths into a museum of cacti in this way was typical of César Manrique's way of working. Farmers had dug this pit by hand around 1850. They had transported the loose volcanic rock to their fields by donkey-cart to protect the fields from drying out. The remaining monoliths could not be removed as the rock was too hard – in those days there were no machines. Today, 1420 species grow here, with a total of 9700 plants. Most of the cactus species come from America, a few come from Madagascar and the Canary Isles. Some of them are fully grown at two to three centimetres, while others such as the caneja gigantea attain heights of twenty-five metres. The most remarkable specimen on show is the euphorbia handiensis, which grows exclusively on Fuerteventura. Open from 9.00–17.00. It costs 700 ptas.

Mirador del Río Mirador means vantage point, look-out, oriel. Mirador del Río is an oriel on the north cap of the island, 479 m high, it stands like an eyrie in solitary splendour above Graciosa. The view across to the islands Graciosa, Montaña Clara and Alegranza is fantastic. It was none other than Manrique who was responsible for the conversion of the former artillery store *Baterías del Río.* However, the idea came from an utopian project by the Madrid architect Fernando Higueras, who wanted to build a village into the mountains above the beach of Famara. It was to be a village with lifts to the beach, small groups of bungalows in the mountain wall and tunnel streets. Manrique felt uneasy about the frequent power cuts in Lanzarote which could be a result and so the project was never carried out. But it did give Manrique the idea for Mirador del Río. He had the mountain dug up, built a restaurant in the valley, had two rounded hill tops created above the great space; they were covered in earth, the grass grew on them. Looking towards the north, one can see the off shore islands through a large panoramic window. If one approaches from the south, either via Haría and Yé, or Arrieta and Yé, the street ends by a wrought-iron emblem, before a wall of hills disguised in natural stone. It is open daily from 11.00–18.45. By going through a short corridor one can get into the great hall, which is made less severe by two of Manrique's sculptures hanging from the twin domes.

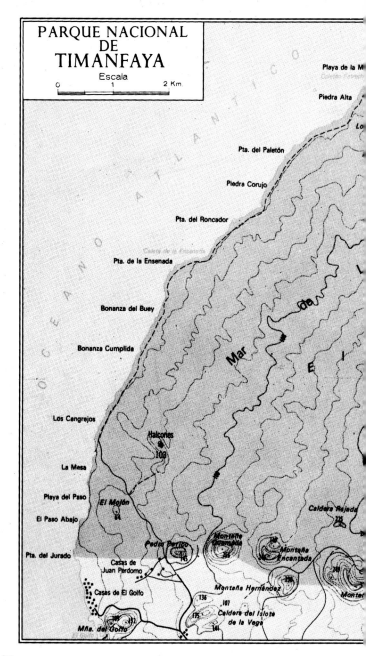

PARQUE NACIONAL DE TIMANFAYA

Escala

0   1   2 Km.

Playa de la M
Piedra Alta
Pta. del Paletón
Piedra Corujo
Pta. del Roncador
Calera de la Ensenada
Pta. de la Ensenada
Bonanza del Buey
Bonanza Cumplida
Los Cangrejos
Halcones
102
La Mesa
Playa del Paso
El Mojón
El Paso Abajo
Pta. del Jurado
Casas de Juan Perdomo
Casas de El Golfo
Mña. del Golfo
Pedro Perico
Montaña Quemada
Montaña Encantada
Caldera Rajada
Montaña Hernández
Caldera del Islote de la Vega
136
107
141

OCEANO ATLANTICO

Mar de E

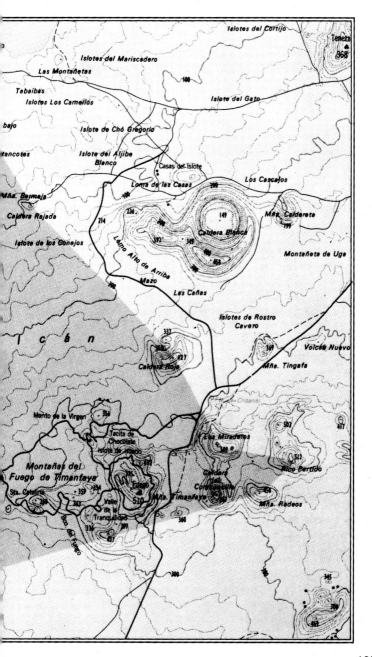

Montañas del Fuego   If one travels 5 km on from Yaiza in the National park, one comes to the Timanfaya, where caravans of dromedaries wait at the foot of the mountains for tourists. From here you can ride into the Fire Mountains and experience the unique "moon landscape". Here you will find all kinds of volcanic manifestations, which were created in the period of eruptions 1730–1736 (see Volcanic Eruptions in the 18th and 19th century, p. 44). It is well worth visiting the Fire mountains just to see the volcanoes' many nuances of colour, their shades changing as the trade wind clouds drift by. You can reach the national park by tour operators bus, taxi or by rented car. It is forbidden to just walk through the park. A few kilometres from the caravans of dromedaries the *Ruta de los Volcanes* begins. From this point on it is necessary to pay an entry fee. It is open from 9.00–16.45. A round trip by bus through the volcanic landscape is included in the entry

fee. The individual volcanic manifestations are explained during this tour. It is two kilometres from the pay booth to the Islote de Hilario. This is the centre of the active volcanic landscape. The earth is hot. By way of demonstration a piece of gorse is put into a natural opening in the earth to a depth of about half a metre – it soon starts to burn. Water that is shaken into metal pipes (which are left in the earth) vaporizes in seconds and shoots out of the earth in fountains of steam. These natural spectacles are performed continously by one of the park employees. The earth's temperature is already 400°C six metres down. The hermit Hilario is said to have lived at the Islote de Hilario for 50 years. His only companion was a dromedary. Hilario is said to have planted a fig tree which never bore fruit, because, according to legend, the blossom could not feed on the flames. Manrique built the *El Diablo* restaurant at the Islote de Hilario; its simple lines mean it is well integrated into the landscape. Only materials such as stone, metal and glass were used due to the high temperature of the earth. From the generously proportioned dining room, one has a wonderful panoramic view right across the volcanoes to the sea. It is a thorough pleasure to while away a little time here. The kitchen is something of a surprise – it is powered, at least in part, by the volcano. A large grill above an opening of about 6 m depth, is powered by the earth's warmth. The reading on the grill is 300°C. The ideal grilling temperature.

Monumento al Campesino   The monument to the hard working and ingenious farmers bears the name: *Fecundidad al Campesino Lanzaroteño* (Fertility for the Lanzarotean Farmers) and stands shortly before Mozaga in the geographical centre of the island. The sculpture, which is 15 m high was designed by Manrique and realized

by J. Soto in 1968. It is composed of former water tanks, wrecked fishing boats and cutters and depicts the farmer with his cattle. The Farmer's House (*Casa del Campesino*) stands next to it; it is a renovated and extended farmstead with which Manrique probably wanted to make a monument to the architecture of the island. A museum, shop and restaurant, serving typical Canary dishes, form a part of this farmstead. It is well worth trying Canary specialities here.

Salinas de Janubio   (see Saltmining or the Salinas of Janubio, p. 68)

Beaches

The coast of Lanzarote measures 194.6 km. There are 87 beaches on this stretch of coastline. 28 of them are white or golden sand, 33 are black sand, the rest are mixed or stoney. Only 36 of the beaches are used for touristic purposes. Six of the beaches are mediumly well frequented, only two are crowded. It is still possible to find a quiet spot. Nude sun bathing is tolerated, but only done on the quieter beaches. Sun loungers, sun shades, surf boards and peddle boats can be hired at the Playa Blanca near Puerto del Carmen (not to be confused with the village Playa Blanca in the south), the island's most crowded beach. Traders sometimes come by with drinks and other things. Bars and restaurants are nearby. You can only reach the quieter beaches by car (or taxi). There are no traders there and you have to take your own food. (*Just one warning* – Don't swim out too far, the currents are unpredictable and can be dangerous. If you want to swim long distances, swim parallel to the coast.)

Playa Blanca by Puerto del Carmen   Is situated in front of the tourist centre of Puerto del Carmen (see above) and is a light, wide sand beach about 2,500 m in length. It is the most popular beach. Bars, restaurants and apartments are not much further than 100 m away. The beach and the water are clean. Towards Playa Quemada, in the south west of Puerto del Carmen, there are small, undisturbed beaches and bays.

Playa Blanca in the south   This is also the name of the fishing village which is gradually becoming a tourist settlement (see above). The beach is actually very small, always quite full, with a nice view across to Fuerteventura. The beach is next to Playa Blanca's bank promenade, where there are many bars and restaurants. The beaches of Papagayo (see above) lie to the east of the village.

Playa de la Cantería   It is the most north easterly beach, situated to the west of Orzola. It is mostly windy and cool. Dangerous current, one should not swim outside the bay.

Playa de las Cucharas   Is situated between the Hotel Las Salinas and the Hotel Teguise on the Costa Teguise (see above).

Playa de Famara   Is amongst Lanzarote's most beautiful beaches. However, there is a continuous strong on-shore wind. Caution is advised when bathing, the current is strong. The coast is suitable for surfing and wave riding. The beach stretches more than one kilometre before the Risco de Famara, a steep cliff wall. The holiday town Famara can be found behind the beach, the village of La Caleta (see above) is situated to the west.

Playa de la Garita   Here on the east coast, to the south and north of Arrieta (see above), there is a series of small beaches, some of which are hard to get to. Here you can be undisturbed. The largest is the Playa de la Garita which is right by Arrieta.

Playa de Janubio   Situated in the south west of the island, near the Salinas of Janubio. This black sand beach is not used much. Be careful of the current!

Playa de Matagorda   Is the continuation of the Playa de los Pocillos (see above). The beach alternates between sand and reefs.

Playas de Papagayo   About 4 km from the village of Playa Blanca (see above) there is a series of sand bays around the Punta de Papagayo, the most southernly point of Lanzarote. The beaches begin at the Punta del Águila, where the Castillo de las Coloradas (see above) stands. The beach here is a little stoney with black sand. The light sand beaches, the most beautiful in Lanzarote begin a little further on after some hills and cliffs. They are flat and the water is as clear as glass. These beaches are the Playa Mujeres, the Playa del Pozo, up to the semicircular bay where fragments of the former village of El Papagayo can still be seen. Drinks can occasionally be bought from a passing goat herd. The beaches can be reached via slopes which are not always easy to find. Although the Papagayos, which are also nudist beaches, are becoming increasingly crowded, it is still possible to find a quiet spot.

Playa de los Pocillos   Situated in front of the urbanisation of Los Pocillos, this beach is the north easterly extension of the Playa Blanca near Puerto del Carmen (see there) and stretches about 2 km. Good for surfing, running and bathing. Less crowded than the Playa Blanca beach.

Playa del Reducto   It is the town beach by Arrecife and is the place where most of the people from the town go. It is very popular in the afternoon and is Lanzarote's only polluted beach.

The Canary Cuisine

It is predominantly in the simple restaurants and country inns, where the natives go, that you will encounter typical Canary cuisine. The Canary people eat well and plentifully. The owners of many hotels and tourist centres have changed to serving international dishes. The restaurants range from coffee houses to steak houses to pizzerias to gourmet restaurants – in other words almost everything one is used to at home. The quality of the food on offer is very varying (see Special Restaurants).

In a *restaurante* the main meals are offered just as they are here. The restaurants and cafeterias are required by law to hang out their menus with the prices of all food and drinks. They also have to make a form for complaints (*hoja de reclamaciones*) available, which can be filled out in every language and must be brought to the notice of the authorities within 48 hours. The restaurants are obliged to offer a reasonable tourist menu. It is made up of a starter, main course and desert and usually includes a choice of a quarter litre of wine or mineral water. Bars are a mixture between a restaurant and pub. *Tapas* are nearly always available there and a full meal is also often available. Bodegas serve only wine.

A breakfast (*desayuno*) speciality is the *huevo pasado*. It is an egg, put into a ladle and dipped just once into boiling water. Hors d'œuvres (*entremeses*) and desert (*postres*) are usually eaten at the main meals *almuerzo* (lunch) and *cena* (dinner) by the Canary people. For snacks between meals there are *tapas*, small canapes. Some bars offer a large range, here are some of the best: chicken in garlic (*pollo al ajillo*), fish in batter (*pescado empanado*), meat balls (*albóndigas*), potato omelette (*tortilla*), tripe (*callos*), goulash (*estofado*), potato salad (*ensaladilla rusa*), octopus (*pulpos*), meat with pulses and tomatos (*ropa vieja*), chick peas with belly of pork (*garbanzos*); sometimes also mussels (*mejillones*), shrimps (*gambas*) and other sea food (*mariscos*) and much more. A delicious and varied main meal can be had by ordering different *tapas*. *Tapa* actually means lid or cover. The notion is thought to have originated in bars which were only allowed to serve drinks. So that hungry drinkers were not lost to restaurants or inns serving food, the owners proffered a *tapa* with every beer (*cerveza*) or glass of wine (*vino*). They were little plates of olives, goat's cheese or a piece of meat which they placed on the top of the glass. You can get almost all the drinks that you are used to in Europe. The local brands of beer are *Tropical* and *Dorada*, the wines from the mainland are recommended, for example from the Rioja region, as are the Canary wines, especially those from El Hierro and Lanzarote. The Canarians drink *ron* (a clear white rum) as an aperitif or vin ordinaire. *Ron con miel* (rum with honey) is particularly nice. The national drink of the Canaries, however, is whisky with mineral water. After the meal one drinks coffee with brandy, aniseed brandy, banana liquer or a *carajillo*. This is a flambéd brandy (sometimes served with sugar, a coffee bean, a slice of lemon, a little coffee liquer or aniseed liquer), which is put out with black coffee. Unfortunately, this fine kind of *carajillo* is rare; in most bars you just get a *café solo* with a little brandy added. The coffee is dark roasted. An espresso is called a *café solo*, coffee with a little milk is called *café cortado*, *café con leche* is the name for a coffee with a lot of milk. You can usually choose which kind of milk you would like: cow's milk (*leche natural*) or *leche condensada* (condensed milk). The mineral waters on offer are good (for example *firgas*); it is good idea to drink a lot of water to compensate for the minerals which are lost in sweat. It is not advisable to drink tap water or well water unless it has been boiled beforehand. The *pilar* is an integral part of every Lanzarotean house. The *pilar* is a cube of muschelkalk and sandstone which has been hollowed out inside. At the bottom the cube has been rounded off. It is hung in a wooden stand, especially made for it. The Lanzaroteños use this stone to collect their well water. The water is purified and enriched with minerals. It slowly drips into a clay cup which stands on a clay saucer, which has a whole in the middle.

This is turn stands on a clay jug, which collects the water as it overflows and keeps it cool. It was a custom earlier to take a sip of water from the clay cup before going into a house. Today the *pilar* is almost only used as a decorative relict. And it really is decorative. After it has been in use for a while, adiantum starts to grow on the stone; it grows very quickly and lusciously. With its lime green leaves and stems that appear to be black and lacquered, like Chinese lacquer, it adorns the *pilar*.

One should not pass on the Canary specialities. As a starter *tapas* or a plate of mixed hors d'oeuvres are the best choice. The latter usually comprises goat's cheese (*queso blanco*), uncooked ham (*jamón serrano*), roast pork (*chicharrón de cerdo*, and *pata de cerdo*), olives (*aceitunas*) and much more. The *potaje canario* is a good vegetable soup, the *potaje de berros* an excellent speciality. It is made from potatoes, pulses, meat and fresh water cress. Where fish is served, you can usually also find an original fish soup, *sopa de pescado*, which contains just about everything that the fishermen brings ashore. Fish is served baked (*a la plancha*), fileted (*filete*) or cooked (*cocido*). *Papas arrugadas, mojo verde* and *mojo rojo* (also called *mojo picón*) is served with it. *Papas arrugadas* are small potatoes, which are

cooked in salt water in their skins and which can be eaten in their wrinkly skins. The *mojo* is a typical Canary sauce. *Mojo* consists of a lot of garlic, olive oil, wine vinegar, six local herbs, green chilli (*mojo verde*) or red chili (*mojo rojo*). *Mojo rojo* is very hot. *Mojo verde* is occasionally served with avocado. If you want to eat fish, it is best to enquire what the catch of the day is. *Cherne* is a typical Canary fish, which is only found in this corner of the Atlantic. The *vieja* (= old woman) is a tasty carp-like Atlantic fish and one of the first fish specialities of the Canary archipelago. It is cooked in its skin and served with oil and vinegar. *Cabrilla* (goat head fish), *pescadilla* (whiting) are delicious, but hard to find. *Mero* (grouper), *Sama* (red brace) and *atún* (tuna) are thoroughly recommended. Sardines feature on nearly all the native menus. Shell fish and sea food are a little trickier – the amount caught is not early enough to cover local consumption. Much of it is flown in deep frozen and this is particularly the case with squid (*calamares*), shrimps (*gambas*), king prawns (langostinos), cray fish (*langostas*) and lobster (*bogavante*). The mussels (*mejillones*) are guaranted to come from the African coast or from the Spanish main land. *Lapas* (limpets), which are caught on Lanzarote's cliffs are fresh, of firm consistency and are often served with *mojo verde*. *Caldo de pescado* is a fish stock (not a soup) made with freshly cooked fish, which is served with sweet potatoes. The *sancocho* is a genuine fish dish. *Sancocho* is made from simmered dried cod with sweet potatoes, onions and garlic. The *cazuela* is a fish stew made from filets of fish, tomatos, onions, garlic and parsley. The south is usually associated with *gofio*. *Cazuela de mariscos* is a sea food stew. *Gofio* was handed down from ancient Canary times and means bread. It is made of roasted corn-, barley- or wheat meal that is put into a goat's skin (*zurrón*) with a little water and kneaded. The *zurrón* is also used to preserve and transport the *gofio*, for example when it is used as food in the fields. A manageable portion is taken from the *zurrón* and it is then rolled back into a ball. *Gofio* is rather dry, therefore the Lanzaroteños drink a lot of wine with it. *Gofio* is particularly tasty when mixed with honey and fruit juice. The natives also serve *gofio* with fish dishes, mix it into fish soups, *gofio escalado*, or stir it into warm cow's or goat's milk or their *café con leche* as an energy-giving breakfast. Sadly, *gofio* can not be found on many menus. *Puchero canario* is an excellent dish, which the natives like to prepare on Sundays or public holidays. At least four types of vegetables are steamed separately in salt water or stock. Different sorts of meat are added to it, such as beef, pork, goat, lamb and game (up to seven different types of meat), resulting in a spicey stock. Other meat dishes which are recommended are: *carne de cochino en adobo* (roast pork which has been laid in a marinade), *cordero* (lamb) with

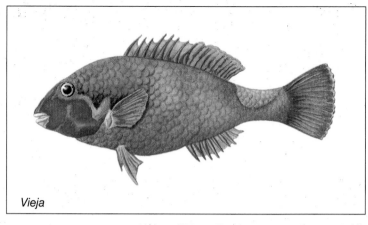

Vieja

Cabrilla

Cantarero

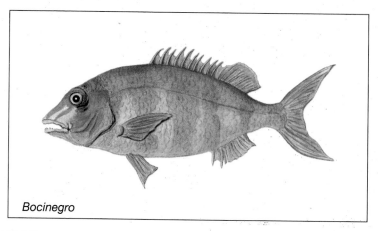

Bocinegro

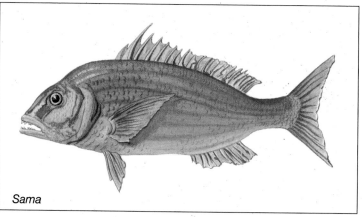

Sama

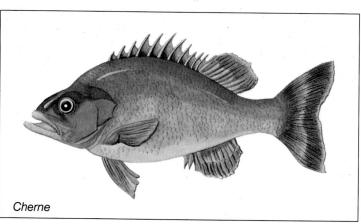

Cherne

mint sauce. Baby goat (*cabrito*) is something else which should not be missed. The baby goats are bred mostly on Fuerteventura. Rabbit (*conejo*) is a further Canary speciality. During the hunting season (first Sunday in August until last Sunday in December: Small game hunting; wild rabbit, wild dove, partridge) the best choice is a wild rabbit (*conejo salvaje*). It is simmered in a meat stock with herbs, chilli, garlic and saffron. *Mojo rojo* is usually served with it.

A Canary native doesn't go without his desert. He usually chooses something good and solid, if he doesn't immediately plump for *flan* (egg custard) with caramel sauce or for melon. *Torrijas* are corn meal cakes with aniseed and honey. *Frangollo* is a sweet dish made from milk and corn, *bienmesabe* a banana dish with almonds, cocoa powder and whipped cream. *Pudín de queso fresco* is a desert made with goat's cheese and eggs. The *bonbon gigante* really is gigantic, at least in calories. It is made from grated chocolate, which is mixed with egg-yolk in a basin above hot water. If you are looking for something lighter, it is best to order fruit (*frutas*). Particularly good is the "Canary" banana, intruduced from Indochina. It is a small species of banana (*musa cavendishii*), which is not sensitive to the weather and is particularly sweet. Figs (*higos*) are served rather less frequently, although they thrive here.

The Canary people eat lunch between 13.00 and 16.00; in the evening they don't usually eat much before 20.00. It is usually noisy and the most important thing is that plentiful quantities of each dish are served up. Everyone can eat what they like; the main thing is that they enjoy it. A lot of wine is drunk with the meal. Toasts are only made on the Canaries at special times of celebration. To find out how to find the individual restaurants and bars, please read the chapter Places – Sights – Beaches, and **Special Restaurants**.

Dictionary of Food and Drink

We have tried to list the regional food and drinks as extensively as possible. Before this there are the rules for pronunciation. You can find more on the Spanish language in the chapter **General Travel Tips:** Language.

Pronunciation

In most cases Spanish is pronounced just as it is spelt. Here are the exceptions:

b is pronounced softly
c in front of i and e is pronounced th (cena-dinner)
ch is pronounced like ch in chair (coche-car)
d on the end of a word is pronounced only slightly or not at all (Madrid)
g in front of a, o, u is hard (like in good)
g in front of e, i is pronounced like a hard ck (Argentina)
gue, gui is pronounced ge, gi (as in Teguise)
güi is pronounced like gui (Güime)
h is not pronounced
j is pronounced like a hard ch (ajo-garlic)
ll is pronounced like ly (paella)
ñ is pronounced like ny (mañana-tomorrow)
qu is pronounced like a hard c (queso-cheese)
r are rolled (pero-but)
rr is stronger (perro-dog)
s is pronounced like a double ss
y at the end of a word is pronounced ee
z is pronounced like a strong th

The vowels are always short. If words have an accent (último), it is always the letter with the accent which is stressed. The stress for words without accents which end in a vowel or n or s (febrero) is on the last but one syllable. If words end in other consonants (metal) the last syllable is given the emphasis.

Food

a caballo: Steak with two fried eggs
acedera: sorrel
aceite: oil
aceituna: olive
achicoria: endive
(al) adobo: marinated
aguacate: avocado
ahumado: smoked
ajiaceite: garlic mayonnaise
(al) ajillo: cooked in oil and garlic
ajo: garlic
a la plancha: baked
albahaca: basil
albaricoque: apricot
albóndiga: burger
alcachofa: artichoke
alcaparra: caper
aliñado: spiced
almeja: venus mussel
almendra: almond
almíbar: syrup
almuerzo: lunch
alubia: bean
anchoa: anchovie, sardine
anguila: eel
angula: baby eel
apio: cellery
a punto: half baked
arenque: hering
arenque en escabeche: salted hering coated in flour
arroz: rice
arroz blanco: white boiled rice
arroz escarlata: rice with tomatoes and shrimps
arroz con leche: rice pudding
asado: roast, roasted
atún: tuna
avellana: hazelnut
aves: poultry
azafrán: saffron
azúcar: sugar
azúcar de uva: glucose
azúcar glass: icing sugar

bacalao (escabeche): dried cod
barquillo: waffle

batata: sweet potato
berenjena: aubergine
berro: (water) cress
berza: cabbage
bien hecho: well done, cooked slowly
bienmesabe: sweet banana desert with almonds
biftec, bistec: beefsteak
bizcocho: sponge cake
bizcocho borracho: cake soaked in rum
bizcotela: biscuit
blando: soft, tender
bocadillo: filled bread
bogavante: lobster
bollito, bollo: bread roll
bonbon gigante: chocolate desert
bonito: mackeral like tuna
brocheta: spit, skewer
budin: desert, mousse
buey: ox, cattle
buñuelo: Viennese whirl
butifarra: special Catalonian sausage

caballa: sort of mackerel
cabeza de ternera: calf's head
cabeza de cerdo: pig's head
cabra: goat
cabrito: kid (young goat)
cabrito en adobo: young goat's meat coated in flour
cacahuete: peanut
cachuela: rabbit ragout
calabacín: zucchini, small pumpkin
calabaza: pumpkin
calamar: calamare, squid
caldo: beef tea, bouillon
caldo de millo: corn stew with pork
caldo de pescado: fish stock with boiled fish
callos: entrails
canela: cinnamon
cangrejo de mar: salt water crab
cangrejo de río: fresh water crab
caracol: snail
carne: meat
carne asado al horno: roast meat
carne a la parrilla: charcoal grilled
carne picada: mince meat
carnero: mutton

carpa: carp
(a la) carta: a la carte
casero: home made
castaña: sweet chesnut
caza: venison
cazuela de cordero: mutton stew
cazuela de pescado: fish stew
cebolla: onion
cebolleta: chives
cena: dinner
centolla: spider crab
cerdo: pork
cereza: cherry
chaucha: green bean
cherne: Canary fish
chicharrón: roast pork
chorizo: pork sausage spiced with
    garlic and paprika
chuleta: cutlet, chop
churros: rolls of pastry baked in oil
cigala: crayfish, king prawn
ciruela: plum
ciruela amarilla: mirabelle
clavo: clove
cocido: cooked, braised/stew of
    potatoes, vegetables and meat
codorniz: quail
col: cabbage
col de bruselas: brussel sprouts
coliflor: cauliflour
colinabo: kohlrabi
comida: food
comino: caraway seed
compota: compote, stewed fruit
conejo: rabbit
confitura: jam, marmalade
congrio: conger
consomé: consomme
corazón de alcachofa: artichoke hearts
cordero: lamb
corzo: deer
crema: cream soup, cream
criadillas (de toro): (bull's) testicles
croqueta: meat or fish croquettes
crudo: raw
crustaceos: crustaceans
cuenta: bill

dátil: date
desayuno: breakfast

dorada: gold brace
dulce: sweet

embuchado: stuffed with meat
embutido: sausage
empanada: meat/fish pate
empanado: cooked in breadcrumbs
emperador: swordfish
enebro: juniper
eneldo: dill
ensalada: salad
ensalada variada: mixed salad
ensaladilla rusa: potato salad
entremés: starter
erizo de mar: sea urcher
(en) escabeche: marinated
escaldón: soup with gofio
escalope: escalope, cutlet
escalope de ternera: veal cutlet
escarola: endive salad
espárragos: asparagus
especia: spice
especialidad de la casa: speciality of
    the house
espinaca: spinach
estofado: braised / goulash / pot roast
estragón: tarragon

faisán: pheasant
fiambres: cold meat platter
fideo: vermicelli
filete: filet
flan: egg custard
frambuesa: raspberry
(a la) francesa: tossed in butter
frangollo: sweet desert of milk
    and corn
fresa: strawberry
fresco: fresh
frío: cold
frito: baked, roasted
fritos de patata: potato croquettes
fruta: fruit
fruta escarchada: candied fruit
fruta del mar: sea food
fruta seca: dried fruit

gallina: hen
gallo: cock, rooster
gamba: shrimp

ganso: goose
garbanzo: chick pea
gazpacho: gaypacho, cold vegetable
  soup
gigote: meat loaf
gofio: roasted corn meal
granada: pomegranate
grande: large
gratinado: browned
grosella: (red or black) current
grosella espinosa: gooseberry
guarnición: side dish
guisado: braised, steamed / stew,
  ragout
guisante: pea

habichuela verde: green bean
hamburguesa: hamburger
helado: ice cream
hielo: ice, ice cube
hierba: spice, herbs
hierbas finas: finely chopped herbs
higado: liver
higo: fig
hinojo: fennel
hongo: field mushroom
(al) horno: baked in the oven
hortaliza: vegetable
hueso: bone
huevo: egg
huevo cocido: soft boiled egg
huevo duro: hard boiled egg
huevo escalfado: poached egg
huevo frito: fried egg
huevo pasado: soft beaten egg, dipped
  once into boiling water
huevo revuelto: scrambled egg
huevo con tocino: egg with bacon

jalea: gelee
jamón: ham
jamón ahumado: smoked ham
jamón cocido (also: jamón de York):
  cooked ham
jamón gallego: smoked, thinly sliced
  ham
jamón serrano: uncooked salted
  ham
jengibre: ginger
(al) jerez: braised in sherry
judía: bean
jugo: sauce / gravy

jurél: kind of mackerel

lacón: shoulder of pork
langosta: cray fish
langostino: king prawn
lapa: limpet
laurel: bayleaf
lecbón: young pig
lechuga: green salad, lettuce
legumbre: peas and beans
lengua: tongue
lenguado: sole
lenteja: lentil
liebre: hare
lima: lime
limón: lemon
lista de platos: menu
lista de vinos: wine list
lombarda: red cabbage
lomo: chine, saddle
lonja: slice of meat

macarrones: macarroni
maíz: corn, maize
manchego: hard yellowish or white
  cheese made from sheep's milk
mandarina: mandarine, tangerine
mantequilla: butter
manzana: apple
marisco: sea food, shell fish
matambre: beef olive
mayonesa: mayonnaise
mazapán: marzipan
mejillón: mussel
mejorana: marjoram
melocotón: peach
melón: melon
membrillo: quince
menta: (pepper) mint
menú: set meal
menú del día: meal of the day
menú turístico: tourist menu
menudillos: innards
merengue: meringue
merluza: hake
mermelada: marmalade
mero: grouper
mezclado: mixed
miel: honey
mixto: mixed, different
mojo picón: spicey sauce
mojo rojo: a hot red sauce

mojo verde: a typical green sauce
molusco: shell fish
mora: blackberry, mulberry
morcilla: black pudding
morilla: moral (mushroom)

nabo: turnip
naranja: orange
nata: cream
nata batida: whipped cream
nuez: nut
nuez moscada: nutmeg

olla: stew, casserole
olla gitana: vegetable stew
olla podrida: meat casserole
ostra: oyster
oveja: sheep

paella: rice dish (Spanish national dish)
palillo: tooth pick
palmito: palm heart
pan: bread
panecillo: bread roll
papas: potatoes
papas arrugadas: potatoes cooked in
  salted water
(a la) parrilla: grilled, roasted
parrilla mixta: mixed grill
pasado: cooked
bien pasado: medium rare, almost
  cooked
poco pasado: rare
pasas: sultanas
pastas: pasta
pastel: cake, pastries
pastel de patatas: potato fritter
pastelillo: small cake
pata: foot
pata de cerdo, pata cochino:
  pigs trotter
patatas: potatoes
patatas fritas: chips
pato: duck
pavo: turkey
pechuga: breast of chicken
pepinillo: spiced gherkin
pepino: gherkin
pepito: bread filled with meat
pera: pear
perca: fresh water perch

percebe: mussel
perdigón: young partridge
perdiz: partridge
perejil: parsley
perilla: a hard mild cheese
perrito caliente: hot dog
pescadilla: whiting
pescado: fish
picadillo: mince
picado: finely sliced
picante: hot, spicey
pichón: dove
pierna: leg
piel: skin, shell
pimentón: ground pepper
pimienta: pepper
pimienta cayená: cayenne pepper
pimiento picante: (red or green) pepper
pincho: kebab
pintada: guinea fowl
piña: pineapple
(a la) plancha: grilled on shelf or platter
plátano: banana
platija: flounder
plato: meal, portion, plate
pollito: small chicken
pollo: chicken
pomelo: grapefruit
porción: portion
postre: desert
potaje: Canary vegetable soup
potaje de berros: (water) cress stew
puchero: meat or vegetable stew
pudin: desert, mousse
puerro: leek
pulpo: octopus, squid
puré de patatas: mashed potatoes

queso: cheese
queso blanco: goats milk cheese
queso tierno: fresh cheese
quisquilla: prawn or shrimp

rabanitos: radish
rábano: radish sauce
rábano picante: horseradish
rallado: grated
raya: ray
rebanada: slice
rebozado: cooked in batter
recargo: supplement

rehogada: sauteed
relleno: filled, stuffed
remolacha: turnip
repollo: white cabbage
requesón: quark
riñon: kidney
róbalo: shellfish
rodaballo: turbot
(a la) romana: cooked in batter
romero: rosemary
roncal: strong hard cheese
rollo: roulade
ropa vieja: meat and vegetable ends
    with tomatoes and pepper
rosbif: roast beef
rosquilla: dough nut
ruibarbo: rhubarb

sal: salt
salado: salted
salchicha: small sausage
salchichón: salami
salmón: salmon
salmonete: red brace
salsa: sauce
salsa blanca: creamy, white sauce or
    mayonnaise
salsa española: spiced wine sauce with
    herbs and garlic
salsa mayordoma: butter sauce with
    parsley
salsa picante: pepper or paprika sauce
salsa verde: parsley sauce
salsifi: viper's grass
salteado: sauteed
salvia: sage
sama: red brace
sancocho: cooked dried cod
sandía: water melon
sardina: sardine
sémola: semolina
sencillo: simple
sepia: cuttle fish
servicio: service
servicio (no) incluido: service (not)
    included
sesos: brain
seta: field mushroom
solomillo: filet, loin
sopa: soup
sopa de fideos: noodle soup
sopa de verduras: vegetable soup

suave: mild
suflé: souffle
suizo: milk roll
surtido: selection

tajada: slice, piece
tallarín: noodle
tapa: canape
tarta: tart, cake
ternera: veal
tiburón: shark
tocino: bacon
tollo: dried, grilled fish
tomillo: thyme
torrija: a small cake made from corn
    meal served with aniseed and honey
tortilla francesa: omelette
tortilla española: potato omelette
tortuga: turtle
tostada: toast
trucha: trout
trufa: truffles
turrón: nougat

uva: grapes
uvas pasas: raisins

vaca: beef
vaca salada: corned beef
vainilla: vanilla
(a la) valenciana: with rice tomatoes
    and garlic
variado: mixed
varios: various
verdura: vegetable
vieira: mussel
vieja: Canary fish
vinagre: vinegar
vinagreta: vinagrette

yema: egg-yolk
yemas: desert made from beaten egg-
    yolks and sugar

zanahoria: carrot
zarzamora: wild blackberry
zarzuela: stew of fish and shellfisch
zarzuela de mariscos: thick soup made
    with sea food
zarzuela de pescado: a fish and shell
    fish dish
zarzuela de verduras: vegetable stew

Drinks

agua: water
agua mineral: mineral water
agua con gas: fizzy mineral water
agua sin gas: still mineral water
aguardiente: brandy
anis: aniseed liquer
anis seco: aniseed brandy

batido: milk shake
bebida: drink
bien frio/-a: well chilled
botella: bottle
media botella: half bottle

caña: small draught beer
carajillo: coffee with brandy
café: coffee
café con leche: coffee with a lot of milk
café cortado: coffee with some milk
café descafeinado: decaffeinated coffee
café granizado: iced coffee
café solo: espresso
café solo largo: double espresso
cerveza: beer
cerveza de barril: draught beer
coñac: cognac, Spanish brandy
con hielo: with ice
cosecha: vintage
crema de cacao: chocolate liquer
champán, champaña: champagne, Spanish sparkling white wine
chocolate: hot chocolade
chocolate con leche: hot chocolade with milk

dulce: fruity, sweet desert wine

espumoso: sparkling

gaseoso: fizzy drink
ginebra: gin
granadina: pomegranate syrup

jugo: juice, fruit tea
jugo de carne: beef tea
jugo de fruta: fruit juice

leche: milk
limonada: lemonade
liquor: liquer

naranjada: orange flavoured fizzy drink

ponche crema: avocat

refresco: refreshing drink
ron: rum
ron con miel: rum with honey

sangría: a punch made with red wine, brandy, orange liquer, sugar, fruit and ice
sidra: cider
sorbete: fruit drink with ice

té: tea
tequila: tequila
tinto: red wine (in Columbia, black coffee)

vermú: vermouth
vino: wine
vino blanco: white wine
vino clarete: rose wine
vino común: table wine
vino dulce: sweet wine or desert wine
vino embotellado: bottled wine
vino espumoso: sparkling wine
vino medio seco: medium dry wine
vino de mesa: table wine
vino del país: vin ordinaire
vino de la peninsula: wine from Spain
vino rosado: rose wine
vino seco: dry wine
vino suave: sweet wine
vino tinto: red wine

xampañ: a sparkling wine from Catalonia

yerba mate: mate tea, Paraguayan tea

zumo (de frutas): fruit juice
zumo de limón: lemon juice
zumo de manzana: apple juice
zumo de naranja: orange juice
zumo de uva: grape juice

Special Restaurants

The restaurants named below offer a wealth of dishes and range from simple Canary inns to gourmet restaurants. Particular attention has been paid to the fish restaurants which are worth visiting. In addition, restaurants serving good solid and international food are listed. All restaurants serve more or less the same Spanish wines. The malvasia, a strong, but delicious country wine is to be drank with caution. You can find out more exact details about Canary cuisine in the corresponding chapter.

Arrieta

The **Restaurante Miguel** is one of the typical fish restaurants of Lanzarote. A wonderful view of the mole and the sea can be enjoyed from the terrace. It is a great place to sit and eat. It is a simple rustic restaurant, which is well visited by the natives. Of course, it is also frequented by tourists travelling around the island on their own initiative. (The owner *Miguel* also rents a few apartments in Arrieta). The usual freshly-caught fish are on offer, prepared in the Canary way (see The Canary Cuisine). The various sauces that are served are delicious. The *pescadilla* from the family of the *meros* is particularly tasty. This is served when in season. The *calamares* and the *langostinos* are also recommended. *Papas arrugadas* and goat's cheese are part of every Canary meal. The restaurant is open from 12.30–21.00. Closed on Monday.

If you travel on past Restaurant Miguel (see above) for about 500 m, towards Punta Mujeres, you will come to the **El Lago** restaurant (on the left hand side). It belongs to the same people as Restaurante Miguel and serves a similar kind of food. There is a nice view of the sea. Charcoal grill. Closed on Monday.

El Golfo

You can find the **Casa Torano** by following the main road to (almost) the end. It is the last but one restaurant in El Golfo, which now has seven restaurants to show for itself. The food here is especially delicious. Not only fish is served, but meat and *paella.* Ask (as usual) for the catch of the day. The view of the surf and of the sunset is an experience. El Golfo remains one of Lanzarote's few original villages. Open from noon to about 22.00. Closed on Sunday.

Haría

You must visit Haría in the valley of the thousand palm trees. Haría is an oasis, seeming like an oriental dream. It is worth spending several hours here, with a glass of country wine, goat's cheese, a couple of olives, or a good meal. **El Cortijo** is the most recommended restaurant in Haría. If you arrive in Haría from the direction of Teguise, you will find an old manor house on the left hand side as you enter the village, which has been converted into a restaurant. Excellent cuisine is on offer. Open from 11.00–22.00.

Orzola

The **Punta Fariones** is another excellent fish restaurant in the most nothernly village of Lanzarote. Both the village and the restaurant are worth a trip. In Orzola, which remains authentic, you can watch them unloading the fishing boats and bringing the fresh fish to the restaurants several times a day. Sea food such as *lapas* (limpets) and *langostinos* are recommended. And they are best washed down by the local Lanzarotean wine. Open from 11.00–22.00. Open every day. There are two longboats which leave twice daily (10.00 and 17.00) for Graciosa (see there). Lanzarote's largest off shore island is well worth visiting.

If you wish to go deep-sea fishing or take a boat to the offshore islands, ask at the restaurant for David. He will take you wherever you wish in his boat Guacimara (up to 25 persons).

Playa Blanca

In Playa Blanca you will find twenty eating places of varying quality. Starting with the usual international cuisine, you can eat Canarian, Italian, French and Chinese. The restaurant **Brisa Marina** is highly recommended. It stands almost in the middle of the promenade, which once belonged to the old and original part of Playa Blanca. You have a splendid view across to Lobos and Fuenteventura, the two nearest islands, from any table. The cuisine offers excellent Canarian and international dishes. Ask for freshly caught fish. Open from 12.00–22.00. No closing day.

The **Casa Salvador** restaurant is situated directly on the white sand beach of Playa Blanca and is well known for its Canary and international cuisine. It is amongst the oldest restaurants, which is of course now frequented by tourists. From the dining room and the terrace there is a view across the beach promenade and the sea. Next to the restaurant there is a bar built in the Canary style. Open every day. The restaurant is ideal for families with children; the restaurant building protects part of the beach from the wind. It is quite possible to spend a whole day here. However, on Sunday the beach is crowded. In the bar you can also get some tapas along with refreshments.

Puerto del Carmen

To make orientation a little easier, we recommend the tourist map *Puerto del Carmen*. We are also including the map reference with the location on the restaurants listed below.

El Patio, a centre for the decorative arts, is situated about half way along the main road between Mácher and Puerto del Carmen (by a wind mill). The centre has a restaurant, well known for its fine

individualistic cuisine and sophisticated atmosphere. The kitchen is open from 13.00–15.00 and from 18.30–23.00. The over 100 year old building has been caringly extended, and has preserved its rustic character. Various shops have been integrated into the estate. Sophisticated and imaginative jewellery, boutiques, works of art, a gallery and a garden centre with a large selection of cactuses and Canarian plants. Open from 10.00–23.00. Closed on Sunday. Tel. 51 05 25.

The tourist centre Puerto del Carmen is growing continuously. Now there are more than 250 restaurants and snack bars. Of course, it is impossible for us to list all of these, for space reasons, so below are just some of them – which does not mean that the others are no good. The restaurants mentioned below are especially good in terms of food and atmosphere.

The **El Tomate** restaurant is situated in the Calle Jameos (C-4). It is one of the few gourmet restaurants in Puerto del Carmen, although it is not thought of as one. The food has a German and international touch. The small, but extensive menu is balanced. The home made sauces are delicious and the portions are enormous – not in keeping with gourmet cuisine at all. There are felt pens and drawing pads for children. It is open from 19.00–22.00. Closed on Sunday. It is best to make a reservation. Tel. 82 62 85.

In Puerto del Carmen, there are pizza bars on almost every street corner. However, here we wish to recommend to you an Italian restaurant with a remarkably good cuisine. At the pizza bar **Italica** (C-22) you can not only obtain a variety of exquisite nudel recipes, but also an unbeatable pizza, cooked in a charcoal oven. Carlos, the restaurant owner learnt his trade in Italy. You will find the pizza bar **Italica** in the first row, opposite the Los Pocillos beach, in the shopping centre of Jameos Playa 66. Open from 9.00. Tel. 51 16 68. Good prices. Pizzas to takeaway.

A cosy and elegant Café is also recommended, where you can have an excellent breakfast: The **Café Christina**. You will find the coffee house, built in the Old Vienna style, in the shopping precinct *Atlántico* (C-9), on the first floor, above the Waikiki. Homemade tarts and cakes, excellent coffee, German bread, extensive breakfast, snacks and cocktails are served. Apart from that, there is also plain cooking. Ask for the day menus. Open from 9.00–23.00.

Teguise

It is worth spending a longer period in this, the former capital of the island. Teguise (see there) is the village in Lanzarote which has the most to offer culturally. It is particularly nice to make a trip on Sunday when the market is held. The **Acatife** restaurant (on the main square opposite the church) is recommended to those who really want excellent food. During the day rustic Canary foot is served; in the evening the finest cuisine: pumpkin soup covered with puff pastry, fish cooked in a crust of salt, rabbit, figs in red wine. The dining rooms should be seen at all costs. Tel. 84 50 37.

Uga

Up in Uga, directly on the main road between Mácher and Yaiza, you will find the excellent and highly recommended smoked salmon works (no. 4). The quality could not be better. You can buy a kilo of the finely smoked salmon, which is imported from Norway or Scotland, for 4,500 ptas. The minimum weight you can buy is half kilo. Open Monday to Friday from 10.00–13.30 and 15.00–18.30, Saturdays from 10.00–14.00. Tel. 830132.

Yaiza

It is the atmosphere of the garden restaurant *La Era* which is so convivial. It was set up in a farmhouse, more than 300 years old which César Manrique restored and converted. The garden, which is planted with indigenous and tropical plants is worth seeing, as is the building and its interior design. Typical Canary cuisine is on offer (see The Canary Cuisine). Especially good are: *cabrito, puchero* and the *potaje de berros*. Open from 12.00–23.00 the whole year round. Open every day. Tel. 830016.

Restaurante La Era in Yaiza

To complete the chapter on the **Special Restaurants** we would wish to give a word of praise for another wine. The **Bodega La Era** presses a classical Malvasier, which belongs to one of Lanzarote's best wines. The grapes, also called the fruit of the volcanos, ripe in the wine-growing area between Uga and La Geria.

"The fruit from the burnt earth. Lanzarote's climate, the volcanos whose fire gave rise to the fields and its good harvests, produced the fruit from the burnt earth. The Conejero wine, a young, fresh and natural wine is the result of wise and very old working methods of our wine-growers and the outstanding quality of the grapes of our island. A masterpiece of wine-growing, which we bottle, so that your critical taste buds are able to enjoy it", write the wine growers. The production is limited. The **Bodega La Era** presses white wine, Rose, Moscatel and red wine. The wines can be obtained in several supermarkets such as Vivó, Marcial and Spar, and in several choice restaurants. You are advised to go directly to the **Restaurant La Era** for wine-tasting. We recommend you take cooked cheese with mojo verde (queso asado con mojo) with your wine, pickled olives (aceitunas), and smoked Cherne, a native island fish (cherne ahumado).

Special Accommodation

Costa Teguise

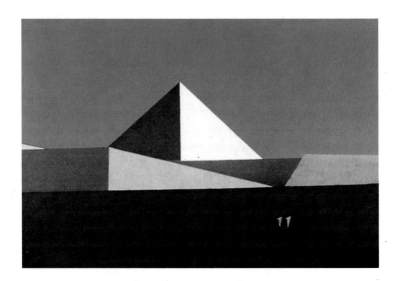

Etora, the holyday and conference centre, is a place of encounter: for encountering one's whole way of looking at things and the one's methods of recognition. This involves, for example, esoteric theory, philosophy, psychology, alternative medicine, creativity and self discovery. There are also a number of experienced, well known consultants and therapists who hold seminars and workshops, like the **Etora-Forum.** They are also available for individual consultations (for example: plotting one astrological chart, respiratory therapy, reiki, foot reflex massage, body massage, tarot etc.). Here you can meet people with the same way of thinking and undergo and envigorating exchange of experiences (the Etora-Bar is open daily from 18.00). There are also events (for outside visitors too). Every day at 9.00 there is a session of Zen-meditation in the pyramid. Every Sunday at 19.00 there is an evening to welcome and inform guests with a subsequent multi-visual presentation on Lanzarote. At 20.30 daily there are selected videos or lectures. **Etora** is located next to the Playa Roca centre. Tel. 59 09 16, Fax 59 09 19.

La Geria

You can also spend your holiday on a former **wine growing estate**, in the best comfort, in the middle of the wine growing region, which has long been a national park. The landscape is exotic and bizarre, the location quiet, with a view of the Fire Mountains. The individual traveller has the choice of two differently sized apartments, which are generously proportioned and built with a conscious attitude towards the environment. They are tastefully integrated into the former estate. The smaller of the two measures 60 square metres and comprises a bedroom, hallway, kitchen/diner, bathroom and terrace. For a reasonable daily price two adults and a child can easily live there. The larger of the two apartments (100 square metres) has two bed rooms, hall, lounge with an open fire place, kitchen, bathroom and terrace. It is a little more expensive and holds a maximum of five people. So that you can get around a hire car is included in the price: an Opel Corsa (Vauxhall Nova), with fully comprehensive insurance and unlimited mileage. You are collected from the airport. You can rent an apartment directly from the owners: La Geria 12, Yaiza.

The **Bodega El Chupadero** is annexed to the wine growing estate. It is open Fridays and Saturdays from 20.00–3.00. A festival with food, music, dancing, an open fire and pleasant company takes place on every full moon. Cordon-bleu by full moon from 20.00. Entry free.

The Special Book

We wish to bring **Lanzarote & César Manrique** to your attention by means of a brochure. The subjects covered by the brochure cover the seven most important sights created by César Manrique: Los Jameos del Agua – Monumento al Campesino – the restaurant El Diablo – Mirador del Río – Castillo de San José – Jardín de Cactus – Fundación César Manrique. The brochure finishes with an article about César Manrique. It was written by Wolfgang Borsich, author of the travel guide. Photographed by Richard Maslonka. 60 pages in three languages with over 60 photographs. Format 21.5 cm × 21 cm. Cost 975 pesetas.

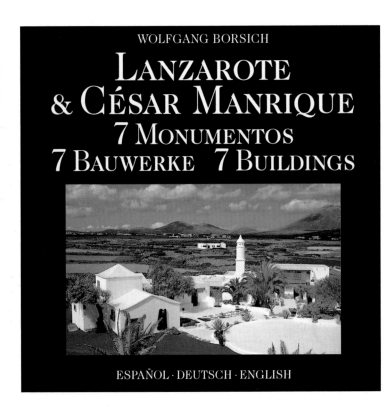

Brief Survey of Puerto del Carmen

Puerto del Carmen is *the* tourist centre of Lanzarote. In order to help you get your bearings in this over-abundance of eating and entertainment places, we are just listing those that we find best. The tourist plan *Puerto del Carmen*, which is very easy to follow, will make it a little easier to find your way. The map also gives you some other tips. To make it even easier we are also including the map reference with the address of the places listed below.

Sport

The **viajes insular** is a sports centre with swimming pool and small snack bar. You can play tennis, fronton, squash and table tennis here. The centre is situated on the *Calle Alegranza* (C-5).

Castellana Sport is situated in *Calle Guanapay* (C-7), Squash, bodybuilding, aerobics, sauna, massage and a snackbar are on offer. Open Mon–Sat 8.00–22.00 and Sun 10.00–21.00.

Shopping

There are shops and shopping centres (*Centros Comerciales*) on every corner. You can shop in supermarkets, boutiques, par-fumeries, duty-free shops, souvenir shops, etc.

It is worth shopping around:
The *Finca del Arte*, **El Patio** is re-commended. About halfway along the main road between Mácher and Puerto del Carmen is a small centre for the decorative arts with a top

restaurant and bar. Various shops have been tastefully integrated into this old renovated farmhouse. Jewellery, clothes, paintings, prints, books, wine, handicrafts and decorative arts are on sale. There is a nursery (for plants) next to the centre. Open from 10.00–23.00.

The **German butcher** is also worth a mention. Situated in the *Avenida de las Playas* (C-8). Good meat and sausage can be bought there. Brown bread, salads and small ready-cooked snacks can also be found.
An instant dry cleaning service can be found in the Calle Juan Carlos I, 25 D (B-5).

The addresses of chemists and doctors can be found in the chapter Brief Information on the Island.

Cafés

The following café is recommended:

Café Christina, this coffee house decorated in the style of Old Vienna is in the *Centro Atlántico* on the first floor above Waikiki. Home made tarts and cakes, excellent coffee, extensive breakfast buffet. Dark grain bread, snacks and cocktails. Open from 9.00–23.00.

Bars

It is difficult to miss the bars in Puerto del Carmen, there are rows of them and there is something for everybody. The **Waikiki** in the *Centro Atlántico* is probably the best (C-9).

Exotic drinks are served amongst other things.

Restaurants

There is no lack of restaurants of varying quality either. See Special Restaurants.

Dancing, Disco Pubs and Discotheques

The **Rock-Café** in the *Centro Atlántico* (C-9), live show. Disco Pub **Paradise** (D-10) in *Avenida de las Playas*.

There are several discotheques such as **Jocker** (D-10), **Tiffany's** (B-15) and **Zeus** (C-7) to choose from. They are open from 21.30.

Music Bars

Apart from folklore, live music is rare on the island. **Bourbon Street** is situated in the *Centro Roque Nublo* (C-3), which plays good jazz every now and again.

Charlie's Live-Musicbar is situated in the *Avenida de las Playas* in the *Centro Atlántico* (C-9). It is on the first floor.

Night Clubs

The **Topless** night club can be found in the *Centro Olivin* (C-4) in the *Calle Juan Carlos I.*

Development of Tourism

Since 1970 the number of visitors to Lanzarote increased twenty-five fold. In 1992 just the province of Las Palmas, which incorporates the islands of Gran Canaria, Fuerteventura and Lanzarote, reveived 3,65 million visitors. That represents an increase of 10 % on the year before or 333,493 more tourists. While 461,337 visited Lanzarote in 1986, 998,094 came in 1992. Lanzarote had the highest rate of increase of all the islands Las Palmas. 353,614 holiday makers visited from Great Britain and Ireland (Great Britain: 345,725, Ireland: 7,889). 124,046 people from Scandinavia visited (Denmark: 11,133, Finland: 45,130, Norway: 26,033, Sweden: 41,750) and 396,273 tourists visited Lanzarote from the Germanspeaking countries (West Germany: 349,700, Austria: 13,321, Switzerland: 33,252). The Spanish tourist industry showed an enormous growth-rate. There were 167,586 tourists in 1992. On the whole though, the tourist curve is progressive. (These figures come from a publication by the "Consejería de Turismo y Transportes de Gobierno Canario". The data was collected in the airports in Gran Canaria, Lanzarote and Fuerteventura.) In 1987 Lanzarote had a capacity to accommodate 33,000 tourists. Originally a capacity for no more than 50,000 tourists was to be approved (the population of Lanzarote is approx. 60,000). According to plans it is possible to accommodate about 300,000 tourists. On the Costa Teguise alone the capacity is supposed to increase to 30,000 by the end of the century. That is larger than the population of a small village (5,000-20,000 inhabitants). In the meantime an approval has been passed for the whole of the island: accommodation for 40,000 more can be built in the next five years.

The Neighbouring Islands

GRACIOSA is the geological continuation of Lanzarote. The two massifs are separated by a 1.5–2 km wide strait called El Río. The name of the island of Graciosa, which is 27 square metres large, means "the graceful" and was given to the island by Jean de Béthencourt. The island is shaped by its four volcanoes, the highest of which is the Pedro Barba (bearded Petrus), measuring 266 m. A little more than 500 people still live very authentically in the villages of Caleta del Sebo and Pedro de Barba. Many of its inhabitants work on Lanzarote. A long boat makes the trip between Orzola in the north of Lanzarote and Caleta del Sebo twice daily (Orzola to Graciosa: 10.00 and 17.00, from Graciosa to Orzola: 8.00 and 16.00). Graciosa is the ideal place for divers, underwater photographers, anglers, dreamers and people in search of peace, sun and sand. The larger part of the island is covered in golden sand dunes and holds much undisturbed beauty. Graciosa is one of the most beautiful places for bathing on the Canary archipelago. By renting a donkey or by jeep (you are driven) you can reach the Playa de las Conchas beach, which stretches for several kilometres on the other side of the island. From there you can see the next island, Montaña Clara. There are no hotels on Graciosa; however, there is a complex of holiday apartments now. You can find simple accommodation in two pensions in Caleta del Sebo. It is best to ask in Orzola at the long boat launch if any there are still any rooms free or you can call 84 00 93, the island's only telephone number, to reserve a room. Fishermen rent out their boats and are glad to give instructions for fishing. You can also make a trip to Alegranza, the most northernly island of the Canary archipelago, which has an ornithological station.

MONTAÑA CLARA (light mountains) is uninhabited. This dead landscape is situated two kilometres north of Graciosa. It is just one km large, with only one volcano, measuring 256 m, no beaches, hardly any vegetation. This island, which is almost entirely covered in pyroclastica, is worthless for tourism (Pyroclastica is the general name for loose volcanic waste such as tephra and tuff).

ALEGRANZA ("joy"), measuring 12 km, is the most northernly island of the Canarian archipelago. It has several volcanoes, the highest measuring 289 m. The earth is covered for the larger part in lava ash and pyroclastica. The coastline is rocky and stoney with little bays. There is an ornithological station and a the island was a former bird paradise. You can make a trip from Graciosa to Alegranza.

ROQUE DEL OESTE (ROQUE DEL INFIERNO) and **ROQUE DEL ESTE** are the tips of volcanoes on the sea bed, which are situated to the north west and east of Graciosa.

LOBOS was named Magi-Mani earlier, and was Béthencourt's refuge. It was certainly once a good hide-out for pirates and slave traders and owes its name to the herds of robbers who stopped here on their voyages. Lobos means wolves and the name refers to the *lobos marinos*, the seals. Most of the island is covered with pyroclastica and its highest point is 122 m. The coastline is rocky, but there are some nice bays for bathing. There is a good area for diving and snorkeling between Lobos and Fuerteventura. A long boat makes the trip from Corralejo (Fuerteventura) to Lobos twice daily. (A ferry leaves Playa Blanca, Lanzarote, for Corralejo three times a day.) Every now and again it is possible to make a trip in one of the private boats – enquire at Playa Blanca harbour for the best information. One family lives on Lobos, and also run it.

SAN BORONDÓN is a dream island: uninhabited, mysterious, an island that roams around and is exempt from tourism. It is said to have surfaced and disappeared again in various places in the Atlantic. It is an island of high mountains and deep valleys, divided by wide rivers. Rivers that are non existant on the other islands and which provide the tropical fauna with water. This island has been known by different names: *Perdida* (the lost island), *Encantada* (the enchanted island) or *Encubierta* (the undiscovered) and is included on medieval maps. According to legend, the Irish monk Saint Brendan (also Borondón) is said to have gone to sea on the back of a giant whale, in search of paradise. The Canary people changed the whale into an island which is supposed to have been spotted in different places. If one approached it, it disappeared. Scientists soberly put it down as a fata morgana.

Brief Information on the Island

This chapter contains information, in alphabetical order, which is specially oriented for Lanzarote. Addresses, timetables etc. can change after going to press and although we obviously try to make the information given here as accurate as possible, we cannot guarantee it. At the time of going to press the information is as current as possible and is updated with every edition. The following chapter **General Travel Tips** gives further useful information. It gives practical information, which is valid for the whole of the Canary archipelago.

See General Travel Tips is abbreviated to (GTT)
See Brief Information on the Island is abbreviated to (BII)

Accommodation

(see Special Accommodation)
If you arrive on the island without pre-booked accommodation you can try to get a room on the Costa Teguise, in Puerto del Carmen and in Playa Blanca. It can be difficult, particularly in high season (August–October, December, January, Easter). You can get a bed in a hotel (pension) for about 2,500 ptas, an apartment for 3–4 people costs between 6,000 and 10,000 ptas per day. The price of hotels is a little below that of European hotels; they are required by law to hang a price list in all the rooms. Be aware that the prices change according to season. Some accommodation:

in Arrecife:
Hotel Residencia Miramar
Calle Coll, 2
Tel. 8104 38
three star

on the Costa Teguise:
Hotel Las Salinas
Tel. 59 00 40
five star

in Puerto del Carmen:
Hotel Los Fariones
Playa Blanca
Tel. 82 51 75

in Playa Blanca:
Apart Hotel
Lanzarote Park
Costa de los Limones
Tel. 51 70 48
three star

Cabildo Insular

147

Air Connections

There are regular scheduled flights between the islands. One should enquire at IBERIA in good time, since the departure times are often changed. La Gomera is the only island not to have an airport and the flight time between each island is about one hour. Flights over the weekend, on public holidays, at holiday times and (above all) during Carnival, are often booked up weeks in advance. To find out about charter flights it is best to enquire at the corresponding travel agency or ask your travel guide.

Airlines

in Arrecife:
IBERIA
Avda. Rafael Gonzales, 2
Tel. 810358
(Information and reservations)

at the airport:
Ticket sales
Tel. 810395

Airport

The airport is seven km south west of Arrecife. If you are not being taken to/from the airport by your tour operator, there are enough taxis (see BII: Taxi). The airport building was designed by César Manrique.

Authorities

in Arrecife:
Ayuntamiento de Arrecife

(Town administration)
Calle Vargas, 10
Tel. 810750

Cabildo Insular
(Island administration)
Calle León y Castillo, 4
Tel. 812508

Delegación del Gobierno
(Passport business)
Calle Cabrera Felipe
Tel. 810188

Boat Connections

There is an ferry between Playa Blanca (Lanzarote) and Corralejo (Fuerteventura). It takes about 45 minutes. Departure from Playa Blanca to Corralejo: daily 8.00, 10.00, 14.00, 16.00, 18.00. Departure from Corralejo to Playa Blanca: daily 9.00, 11.00, 15.00, 17.00, 19.00. You can take a trip in a converted fishing boat from Corralejo to Lobos, Fuerteventura's off shore island.

There is a motor boat from Orzola to Graciosa: daily 10.00 and 17.00. From Graciosa to Orzola: 8.00 and 16.00. If the seas are rough the long boat will not leave.

There are many boats travelling between the various Canary Islands. The largest agency is the Compañia Trasmediterránea (see BII: Boat Agencies). Boats leave for Gran Canaria and Tenerife several times a week, twice a week for Fuerteventura and once a week for Cádiz. You can get to the islands of La Palma, El Hierro and La Gomera from Tenerife.

Trasmediterránea
Calle José Antonio, 90
Arrecife
Tel. 811188
(Information and ticket sales)

Chemists

In Arrecife you can find a chemist in Calle León y Castillo, in the Costa Teguise next to Los Zocos Club, in Puerto del Carmen in the old town, in the Centro Bajamar and near the Chafari apartments, in Tías in the middle of the village and in Yaiza on the thoroughfare, and in Playa Blanca. Chemist is *farmacia* in Spanish and is signposted by a red or green cross. The emergency services alternate. Details of services on Sunday and during the night are listed on every chemist's window (*Farmacia de Guardia*). They are open the usual business hours: Mon-Fri 9.00–13.00 and 16.00–19.00, on Sat 9.00–13.00. Those insured under the NHS (or state medicine scheme) only have to pay a contribution towards costs if they can show a medical insurance record card (*talonario*). A medication for something is called *un medicamento contra*. Below are some illnesses and their Spanish counterpart:

chill: *resfriado*
cold: *catarro nasal*
constipation: *estreñimiento*
diabetes: *diabetes*
diarrhoea: *diarrea*
indigestion: *trastornos*
influenza: *gripe*
insect bite: *picados de insectos*
insomnia: *insomnio*
headache: *dolores de cabeza*
heartburn: *ardor del estómago*
nausea: *náusea*
rheumatism: *reumatismo*

sea sickness: *mareo*
sore throat: *dolores de garganta*
stomachache: *dolores de estómago*
sun burn: *quemadura solar*
sun stroke: *insolación*
tonsillitis: *amigdalitis, anginas*

Some medicines and pills
aspirin: *aspirin*
bandage: *venda*
cardial stimulant: *remedio circulatorio*
charcoal tablets: *pastillas de carbón*
condom: *preservativos*
cough syrup: *jarabe pectoral*
dressing material: *vendajes*
eye drops: *gotas para los ojos*
fever relief drug: *antipirético*
gauze bandage: *venda de gasa*
laxative: *laxante*
ointment: *ungüento*
sedative: *calmante*
sleeping pill: *somnifero*
sticking plaster: *esparadrapo*

Chemists Addresses

in Arrecife:
Farmacia Tenorio
Calle León y Castillo, 41
Tel. 811072

in Puerto del Carmen:
Farmacia Correa Rijo
Urbanisation Chafari
Tel. 825398

in Teguise:
Farmacia Villa Teguise
Plaza de San Francisco
Tel. 845284

in Yaiza:
Farmacia Ortiz Garcia
Plaza de los Remedios, 10
Tel. 830159

Doctors

It is possible to consult good doctors, but it is sometimes difficult. If you are dependent on some medicaments, it is better to take a supply with you. It is also worth taking a travel drug kit with you with pills for travel sickness, sun burn, headaches, diarrhoea and the like. In Arrecife and Puerto del Doctors Addresses and Hospitals). It is not neccessary to have vaccinations before you leave. Injections are not done by doctors, but by their assistents (*practicantes*). In the case of emergency, your travel guide or hotel reception will help you find a doctor.

It is usual for a member of the family to be present if a longer period in

Carmen there is Dr Marin's clinic with an ambulance and dentist (see BII: hospital is necessary (see GTT: Medical Insurance).

Doctors Addresses

in Arrecife:
Centro Dental
Calle Coronel Valls
de la Torre, 6

Clínica Dr. Marín
Avda. Fred Olson, 5
Tel. 81 54 61
9.00–14.00 and 16.00–22.00

in Playa Blanca:
International Clinic
Dr. Manuel Medina Herrera
Tel. 51 70 92

in Puerto del Carmen:
ENGLISH SPEAKING DOCTOR
Praxis Dr. Mager, Avda. de las Playas 37, Tel. 51 26 11, Fax 51 24 44
The doctor speaks English, German, Spanish and French.
Open all the day.

Clínica Dr. Mager
Centro Olivin
Corner Calle Jameos/Botabara
Tel. 825452

German physiotherapist and spiritual
healer
André Geiger
Treatment of backbones and
illnesses of the joints, medicinal
massages.
Monday to Friday 9.30–13.00 and
17.00–21.00.
Calle General Prim, 30
Tel. 511646

Vet:
Clínica Veterinaria
Calle Fred Olsen, 8
Arrecife
Tel. 814650

Emergency Services

Fire brigade (*Bomberos*)
Tel. 814858

Police (*Policía*)
Tel. 091

Guardia Civil
Tel. 811100

Policía Municipal
Tel. 092

Red Cross (*Cruz Roja*)
Emergencies: Tel. 812222

Accident or Emergency Ward
(Casas de Socorro)
Tel. 812222

(see BII: Doctors Addresses,
Hospitals)

Pavilion in the Parque Municipal

British Consulate:
Luis Morote 6–3 (Sapartado 2020)
Puerto de la Luz
Las Palmas
35007 Gran Canaria
Tel. (928) 26 25 08 / 12 / 16
Telegrams: "Britain Las Palmas"
Telex: 95276/answerback 95276
BRTLP)

In case of car breakdown/accidents contact your car rental company. It is worth checking the procedure at the time of renting the car.

Exhibitions, Museums

in Arrecife:
Castillo San José
Museo de Arte Contemporáneo
open: 11.00–21.00

Museo Arqueológico
Castillo San Gabriel
open: Monday to Friday 9.00–14.45

El Aljibe Gallery
Calle José Betancort, 33
open: Monday to Friday 10.30–13.00
and 17.00–21.00

in Tahiche:
Fundación César Manrique
open: Monday to Friday 10.00–19.00
Saturday and Sunday 10.00–14.00

in Villa Teguise:
Palacio de Espínola
open: Monday to Saturday
9.00–15.00, Sunday 9.30–13.00
closed an Wednesday

Los Jameos del Agua:
Museo de vulcanología
open: 11.00–18.45

Fiestas-calendar

This calendar lists the main days of the most important religious and folkloric village festivals. These village festivals usually begin about 10 days before the main day and end about two or three days after (see GTT: Public Holidays).

15 May
Uga: Fiesta de San Isidro
24 May
Montaña Blanca: Fiesta de la Maria Auxiliedora
13 June
Güime: Fiesta de San Antonio
24 June
Haría: Fiesta de San Juan
7 July
Femés: Fiesta de San Marcial del Rubicon (patron saint of the island)
16 July
Teguise and Puerto del Carmen, Tías, Famara, Playa Blanca: Fiesta de la Virgen del Carmen
24 August
San Bartolomé: Fiesta de San Bartolomé
25 August
Arrecife: Fiesta de San Ginés
30 August
Haría: Fiesta de la Santa Rosa
8 September
Yaiza: Fiesta de la Virgen de los Remedios
14 September
Guatiza: People's festival
15 September
Tinajo: Fiesta de la Virgen de los Volcanes
7 October
Arrecife: Fiesta de la Virgen del Rosario
30 November
Tao

4 December
Maguéz: Fiesta de Santa Bárbara
24 December
Teguise: Fiesta Rancho de Pascua

Hiking

Lanzarote is not an island much suited to hiking. It is not just the difficult terrain which gives the hiker trouble, but also the scorching sun and the wearing winds. There are no actual hiking paths. Hiking is forbidden in the Fire Mountains (the national park). In the north there is a footpath from La Caleta along the steep coast. The west coast is charming.

Hospitals

in Arrecife:
Hospital General de Lanzarote
Carretera Arrecife-Tinajo km 1,300
Tel. 80 17 52 / 80 16 36 / 80 19 30

Hospital Insular
Calle Juan de Quesada
Tel. 81 05 00

Veterinary Clinic
Clínica Veterinaria
Calle Fred Olsen, 8
Tel. 81 46 50

in Puerto del Carmen:
Clínica Dr. Mager
Corner Calle Jameos/Botabara
Tel. 82 54 52

César Manrique and Pollo

153

Information

Tourist office of the island administration
Calle León y Castillo, 2 and 4
Arrecife
Tel. 813792

Tourist information
Parque Municipal, Arrecife
Tel. 811860
open 10.00–12.30 and 16.00–18.00
(Not always occupied)

Telephone Directories
– national 003
– international European 9198
– international outside Europe 9191

Inhabitants

About 60,000 inhabitants live on an area of 795 square kilometres, 30,000 of them live in Arrecife. This is a medium density of population of around 75 inhabitants per square kilometre.

Lost Property

The Policía Municipal is responsible for lost property (see BII: Police).

Petrol Stations

Most petrol stations are closed on Saturday afternoon and Sunday and public holidays. The price of petrol is cheaper than in Europe. There are petrol stations in Puerto del Carmen and Tías, between San Bartolomé and Mozaga, in Arrieta, Arrecife, Mácher, Yaiza, Playa Blanca and in Tinajo. 24 hour service only available in Arrecife.

Police

The *Guardia Civil* is the country and criminal police. They are responsible for fighting crime, but they sometimes deal with traffic police matters. Green uniform, black patent helmet.

in Arrecife:
Calle El Jupiter, 2
Tel. 812200

Haría: Tel. 835252
San Bartolomé: Tel. 520712
Tías: Tel. 825266
Yaiza: Tel. 830117

The *Policía Municipal*, the town police, is in charge of traffic and local matters. Every political community has its *Policía Municipal*, mostly in blue uniform.

in Arrecife:
Calle Academia, 3
Tel. 811317

Haría: Tel. 835252
San Bartolomé: Tel. 520712
Teguise: Tel. 840262
Tías: Tel. 825301
Tinajo: Tel. 840021
Yaiza: Tel. 830102

The *Policía Nacional* is national and is under the control of the Spanish Ministry for the Interior. They are responsible for residence and work permits, as well as "lost" notices. The uniform is khaki with a dark brown beret.

in Arrecife:
Calle Coll, 5
Tel. 812350

Post

The main post office and telegramme office is in Arrecife: Correos y Telégrafos, Avda. Gral. Franco, 8. Tel. 80 06 73. Open Monday–Saturday 9.00–14.00.
Telegrams can be collected until 20.30. To send a telegramme by telephone: Tel. 22 20 00. Post office is *correo*, letter *carta*, post card *postal*, stamp *sello.* You can find out the various postal charges by looking them up on the list hanging in the post office. You can also have your mail franked and sent out by the hotel reception (see GTT: Phoning).

Sports Centres

Aeroclub de Lanzarote
Flying Club
at the airport
Tel. 81 14 50

Golf club
Costa Teguise
At the Hotel Salinas
18 hole course
Tel. 59 05 12

Taxi

Taxis can be recognised by the sign SP, *Servicio Publico* (public service) on their green light on the roof of the car when they are for hire and by the taxi adverts which are also on the car roof. Every taxi driver has to carry a list of fares with him, that you can have a look at. The price is made up in units. At present one kilometre costs 94 ptas, one hour waiting time costs 1,300 ptas. A tip of about 5–10% is normal. The minimum fare is 300 ptas.

Tourist Office and Tourist Information

You will find the tourist office in Arrecife:
Calle León y Castillo, 2 and 4
Tel. 8137 92

There is a pavilion on the coastal promenade in Arrecife in the Parque Municipal. You can sometimes get free guides, maps and a list of events. Open from 10.00–12.30 and 16.00–18.00. Unfortunately the pavilion is not always occupied.

Yacht Harbours

There are mooring possibilities for boats by Orzola, on the Costa Teguise, in Arrecife harbour, at the Punta Tiñosa by Puerto del Carmen and in the Playa Blanca harbour. A new yacht harbour has been created between Puerto del Carmen and Playa Quemada: Puerto Calero. Next door is an urbanisation with villas, shops and restaurants. Boat services etc. Tel. 81 69 03.

General Travel Tips

In contrast to the Brief Information on the Island, these general travel tips are valid for the whole of the Canary archipelago. They contain the most important information for travellers.

General Travel Tips is abbreviated to GTT.
Brief Information on the Island is abbreviated to BII.

Architecture

Today the architecture has been europeanised and modernised, especially in the tourist centres and urbanisations. Classic Canary architecture is a simplified variant of Andalusian baroque.

Authorities

The authorities are very busy, expect to have to wait some time and you don't always get the right information. The *Cabildo Insular* (administration of the island) is helpful, as is the *Policía Municipal*. The *Guardia Civil* is responsible for accidents, thefts and the like.

Banks and Exchange Offices

Banks give a better rate of exchange than exchange offices or hotel receptions. Eurocheques can be written to a maximum of 25,000 ptas. Banks are open Mon–Sat 9.00–13.00. In tourist centres there are also odd banks and exchange offices which are also open in the afternoon.

Bathing

The temperature of the water varies over the year between 18 and 24 degrees Celsius. The currents are sometimes dangerous and you are advised to swim along the coastline, never far out. Nudist bathing is tolerated on some beaches, it is not actually allowed by Spanish law (see Places – Sights – Beaches). Do not underestimate the sun's power, especially on the first few days. The refreshing trade winds mean that its effects are not always obvious.

Camping

You can camp anywhere except for those places where it is expressly forbidden – for instance very close to monuments or historical buildings. On the main streets a minimum distance of 50 m must be kept. The Canary people like to camp in the wild. At present there is only one camping site on Gran Canaria.

Car Rental

There are car rental firms on all the islands and in all the holiday villages. They offer small cars, medium range saloons and cross country vehicles. Before signing the contract, make sure that the vehicle is in a road worthy condition. Check the spare wheel which is often missing or faulty and check for any accident damage. Fully comprehensive insurance (about 600 ptas per day) is usually obligatory – if the accident is classed as your fault, your personal excess will probably be around 40,000 ptas. Apart from on Fuerteventura, where basically only the first 100 km are free, no charge per km is made on the other islands. You can get a car from about 2,500 ptas upwards (per day) with the price inclusive of rental, insurance and tax at 4%. There are graduated prices for one day, three days, one week. You have to be at least 23 to be able to drive a rented car. You can also rent motorbikes and mopeds (helmets are obligatory) although these are rarer. It is also possible to rent bicycles, but the strong north east trade wind can take the fun out of a bicycle ride (see GTT: Driving).

Catholic Centre

Puerto de la Cruz de Tenerife
Haus Michael
Calle San Antonio, 36. Tel. 38 48 29

Children

As in Spain, people like to see children on the Canary Islands. You can buy babyfood and nappies in every supermarket. Hotels, restaurants and bars will be glad to warm your bottle. The hotels and tourist centres have facilities for entertaining children.

Consulates

(see GTT: Embassies)

Credit Cards

Hotels, some restaurants and shops accept credit cards (like American Express, Visa, Diners Club, Euro-card, Access etc). Eurocheques are not always accepted.

Customs

Generally there is no custom control on arrival in the Canary Islands. The undernamed goods may be imported tax-free from EEC countries, as long as they are not purchased from duty-free shops. Travellers who wish to import more than the list below do not have to pay duty when they are able to prove it is for their own private use (i.e. family celebrations).

	EEC countries	other countries
Alcoholic drinks (aged 18)		
Wine	90 litres	2 litres
or Spirits under 22%	20 litres	2 litres
or Spirits over 22%	10 litres	1 litre
Cigarettes and Tobacco (aged 18)		
Cigarettes	800	200
or cigarillos	400	100
or cigars	200	50
or tobacco	1000 g	250 g

Drinking Water

Tap and well water is not suitable for drinking without boiling it beforehand. You can buy mineral water in most supermarkets. You should try to drink a lot of it to compensate for the loss of fluid (through sweating). Water is in short supply on all the islands, especially Lanzarote, Fuerteventura and El Hierro. You are asked to use it sparingly.

Driving

If you are travelling to the islands with your own car, a national drivers licence (or a European one), green card (certificate of international insurance), bail bond and the symbol of national identity, which should be fixed to the car, are necessary. You should also remember to have your head lights adjusted (by deflecting the beam) to suit continental driving. In Spain third party insurance is only valid for personal injuries and you should be aware of this when renting a car. (see GTT: Car Rental). The main roads on the islands are all in good condition, in some places, however, they can no longer cope with the density of traffic. Away from the traffic, there are gravel roads and sometimes roads that only jeeps can cope with. If you breakdown, you can get help from the *Policía Municipal* inside the towns and from the *Guardia Civil* in the country. It is forbidden to tow a car away with another car. Disregard for the ban on overtaking or of the speed limit is rewarded by a stiff fine. On A roads the limit is 90 km/h, in built up areas the limit is usually 40 km/h. It is obligatory to wear a seat belt. Apart from the fact that they drive on the right, traffic regulations are not a lot different in Spain. In Spain the weaker always has right of way and traffic coming from the right has priority, even at roundabouts. You should hoot before going round blind bends and before overtaking. The car in front will often signal his intention to turn with hand signals; stretching the arm out horizontally means left, stretching the arm out vertically means right.

Driving Licence and Papers

A national drivers licence (or a European one) is valid for 3 months on the islands. If you are taking your own car you will also need your car registration documents and green card (insurance) (see GTT: Driving).

Electricity

Voltage on the islands is usually 220 volts with two-pin plugs. On some of the smaller islands voltage is sometimes only 110–125 volts. Power cuts are part of every day life.

Embassies

Spanish Embassies
(*Embajados de España*)
in UK:
24 Belgrave Square
London SW1X
Tel. 0712355555
in the Republic of Ireland:
(Spanish Consulate)
17A Merlyn Park
Ballsbridge
Dublin 4
Tel. (1) 691640 / 692597

Consulates on the Canary Islands:
British Consulate
Luis Morote 6-3 (Sapartado 2020)
Puerto de la Luz

Las Palmas
35007 Gran Canaria
Tel. (928) 262508 / 12 / 16
There is no Irish Consulate on the Canaries

Entering the Country – Conditions

You will need your passport to enter the Canary Islands. You may stay for a maximum of 3 months. Vaccinations are not necessary. If you want to take your cat or dog with you will need a proof of injections against rabies and a report on its health by an official veterinary surgeon, which must be attested by the Spanish consulate. The injection against rabies must have been done at least 30 days ago and no more than a year ago. There are no customs controls.

Evangelical Centre

Puerto de la Cruz de Tenerife
Villa Tinguaro
Carretera Taoro
Tel. 372415

Excursions

You can make excursions on and from all the islands: tours of the island, photo- and jeep safaris, day trips by boat, deep sea fishing, folklore evenings, trips to the neighbouring islands for one day or more or a day trip to Morocco. These excursions are organised by the local travel agencies or tour operators. Package holiday makers are usually told about them as part of the information given to them on arrival.

Fauna and Flora

In contrast to the vegetation, there are not many different species of fauna on the islands. The wild dogs – from which the name of the archipelago is supposed to be derived – are of course not here any more. Today the *podenco*, the Pharoah dog is bred and used as a hunting dog for small game. It has long legs, with a long pointed snout, pointed batlike ears. Its coat is short in different tones of brown. It resembles the Arabian greyhound. Donkeys and mules are used as pack and draught animals, in the eastern islands dromedaries are also used. There are herds of goats and – rather more infrequently – sheep on all the islands. The muflon (a kind of mountain goat) is peculiar to Tenerife and La Palma. On Fuerteventura the striped squirrel is threatening to become a regional nuisance. Apart from rabbits, bats and hedgehogs there are not really any larger wild animals. There are no poisonous snakes and dangerous insects on the island. There are many endemic species of insects for insect lovers. The brimstone butterfly and the red admiral are the most conspicuous of the butterflies. The Canary Islands are a winter stopping place for migratory birds. Here you can watch swallows, swifts, larks, the hoopoe, finches, bitterns, shrikes, stonechats, falcons, bustards, sea eagles, sea gulls, vultures and many other birds besides. Indigenous species include the Canary sandpiper and so-called Canary birds, which are named after the island. They are a frequent sight by water or in woods, they are grey-green and can sing only moderately well. The splendidly colourful singing bird commonly taken for the real Canary bird was bred in the German Harz mountains. Something of a living fossil can be seen on the island of Hierro – the 60 cm long lizard *Lacerta simonyi*, which dates from the Tertiary Age. The largest species of lizard is found on Gran Canaria, the *Lacerta stehliniï*. It is endemic to the area and measures about 80 cm. Occasionally a slow worm, the small European legless lizard, can be spotted. Because of their shape they are often mistaken for snakes. For the underwater animal world see Fishing. GTT: Sport: Deep sea fishing and Driving.

The flora on Lanzarote is very varied and it is not possible to mention all plants, so we are restricting ourselves to the most important. If you would like more extensive information on the flora, there is an excellent book "Wild Flowers of the Canary Islands" by David and Zoe Bramwell (published by Stanley Thornes in paperback, 1984) which has a great deal of information as well as clear line drawings and colour photographs. Our brief survey of the fauna is divided into two sections: endemic species – plants which only grow on this latitude and tropical and subtropical plants from other countries. Of the 2,000 species of plants which grow on the Canary Islands, about 30% are endemic.

Endemic plants:
Canarian canariensis (*Canary bell flower*) flowers between January and April, has a gold red bell-shaped flower.

Crassulaceen (*Aeonium*) is a member of the succulent plant family, also known as the house leek. There are fifty different types growing on the islands, in rocky landscapes. The leaves are often edged with red.

Dracaena draco (*dragon tree*) is amongst the oldest trees in the world and is typical of the archipelago. It is closely related to the different kinds of Yukka and is a member of the lily family. The tree has no annual rings; the age of it can be estimated, rather unreliably, by counting the number of branches, which don't always grow at the same intervals of time. The oldest specimen is in Icod on Tenerife; the inhabitants declare it to be 2,500 to 3,000 years old. "Dragonblood" was used to mummify the dead and in the production of ointments. "Dragonblood" refers to the resinous excretion, at first colourless, which emerges when the tree trunk is cut. When exposed to the air it turns dark red.

Echium wildpretii (*Tajinaste*) only grows in the Caldera de las Cañadas on Tenerife. In June it produces a candle-like sprout, which can grow to a height of 2 m and contains more than 80,000 blossoms.

Erica arborea (*tree heather*), called *brezo* in Spanish, is similar to the heather which grows in the temperate latitude. Growing to a height of 20 m, the trees have white or pink flowers. It grows at an altitude of over 800 m, sometimes only as a shrub or mini-shrub.

Euphorbia canariensis (*Euphorbie candalabra*) *cordones* in Spanish, is

Dragon tree

Phoenix canariensis

a spurge plant with poisonous juice, the edges are thorny and the trunks grow like pillars.

Euphorbia regis-jubae, called *Tabaiba* in Spanish, has cactus-like trunks, which resemble pillars and grow to a height of 1.5 m. The shrub is a sort of spurge, its milky juice is poisonous.

Laurus canariensis (Canary laurel tree). On Gomera the trees grow to a height of 20 m. The leaves are pointed and eliptical and are sometimes used as cooking herbs. However, they are not as aromatic as the bay leaf from southern Europe.

Phoenix canariensis (*Canary date palm*) with its slim trunk and branches that curl over it is one of the most beautiful specimens of the palm family. It has spread from the Canaries to the whole of the Mediterranean. It is related to the North African-Arabian date palm, but its golden yellow fruit is not edible.

Pinus canariensis (*Canary pine*) grows on all the islands apart from Lanzarote and Fuerteventura. It grows at an altitude of 1,000–2,000 metres and is the archipelago's most important tree. The hard reddish heart wood is used for building. The conquerors cleared whole forests and used the wood for building ships, fueling the sugar refineries or for the resin and pitch available in the trees. The pine tree grows to a height of 30 m and has a large round top. Its pliable needles, which are grouped together in threes measure 30 cm. Water from clouds and mist condenses on the needles and falls as precipitation. Tests have shown

Tajinaste

that 1,500 more litres of precipitation falls per year and per square km due to the fully grown pines, than in the treeless areas a few metres further away. Hence, the pine trees which need less for their own consumption than they produce, play a crucial role for the water supply.

Rocella tinctoria (*Dye lichen*), called *orchilla* in Spanish. Was important even in the times of the Phoenicians for its red dye.

Viola Cheiranthifolia (*Teide violet*) also called Violeta del Teide or volcanic violeta, it a botanic speciality. It only grows on the dry pumice stone slopes of the Teide up to an altitude of 3,600 m.

Plants from other countries:
African tulip tree (*Spathodes campnulata*) comes from tropical Africa. From January to May this evergreen bears orangey red bell-shaped flowers, which grow in clusters.

Strelitzia

Agave. There are various sorts, but they all have the fleshy leaves ending in a long thorn in common. The leaves are grouped into rosettes. The plants sprouts layers (shoots) from its roots and from the stem. After 8–16 years a flowering shoot grows out of the middle. It can grow up to 12 m high and forms a bough at the end where yellow green blossoms grow. In Mexico the **Pulque-agave** (*agave salmiana*) is used to make the Pulque drink and

Banana

Papaya tree

the **Sisal-Agave** (*agave sisalana*), which is grown in South America, and Fuerteventura, for the fibre produced from the leaves. Rough materials are produced from these fibres such as ropes and sacks.

Avocado tree (*Persea gratissima*) known for its pear shaped fruit, called *aguacate* on the Canaries, they are used for starters and salads. The leaves are evergreen, the flowers whitish yellow, open pinacles.

Banana (from the *Musa cavendishii* family), introduced by the Portuguese from Indochina, it is one of the most important cultivated plants on the archipelago and is still imported. It can grow up to an altitude of 300–400 metres. The annual plants forms a club-shaped inflorescence. In 4–6 months the bananas are ripening. One plants weighs about 30 kg. Once the fruit has been formed, the plant dies, but not without producing new shoots. The strongest of these shoots be-

comes the basis of next year's plant.

Bougainvillea (*Bougainvillea spectabilis*) the climbing plant which comes from the South Pacific is seen often on the islands. It has yellowish flowers on three upper leaves, which can be red, white, yellow, orange and violet.

Eucalyptus tree (*Eucalyptus globulus*) comes from Australia. There are about 20 different types on the archipelago. Wood and ethereal oils are gained from this rapidly growing tree. Its silvery suspended leaves are formed so that they are not exposed to much sunlight.

Fig cactus (*Opuntia ficus-indica*), also called opuntia, it was introduced from Mexico in the 16th century. Its fruit is edible. Cochineal beetles are still bred today on its green shovel-like leaves. An analine red dye is gained from its larva which is used in the production of lipsticks, for colouring aperitifs and oriental carpets.

Poinsettia

Hibiscus (*Hibiscus rosa-sinensis*), also called chinese rose mallow, comes from South China and flowers the whole year round. The one-day flowers are funnel-shaped with a far protruding pistil with many stamens. The flowers are red, yellow and pink.

Oleander (*Nerium oleander*) very poisonous plant, originating from the Mediterranean. This shrub, which can grow to the size of a tree, produces white, red, pink or yellow flowers.

Papaya tree (*Carica papaya*), also called melon tree, comes from tropical America and is cultivated for its fine tasting yellow melon-like fruit.

Parrot plant (*Strelitzia reginae*) also called Strelitzia, comes from South Africa and bears a flower which resembles the head of a bird. The flower is blue yellow with some orange and violet. It flowers the whole year round and is popular as a souvenir.

Poinsettia (*Euphorbia pulcherrima*) known in Europe as a pot plant popular at Christmas time. It is easily distinguished by its red upper leaves. It can grow to a height of 4 m.

In addition to the Canary palm (*Phoenix canariensis*) there is the cocus and king palm, the washingtonia and other sorts. There are a number of fruit trees such as almond trees, orange trees, lime trees, lemon trees, pomegranate trees. There are also apples, pears, and grapefruit, pepper bushes and cinamon trees. There are solitary cork oaks, ombus, cedars, aspens; more frequently there are mimosas and mock rubber trees.

Fishing

(see GTT: Sport)

Flights back

The times of charter flights back are often changed at short notice. For this reason it is better to check with your tour operator at least three days before your departure.

Foreign Exchange

Spanish currency is used on the Canary Islands. The peseta (pta) is only theoretically divided into centimos. 100 ptas is about 60 p. There are 1, 2, 5, 10, 25, 50, 100, 200 and 500 ptas coins and bank notes for 1,000, 2,000, 5,000 and 10,000 ptas. You may take 100,000 ptas into the country, but take only 20,000 out. You may take in other currencies in an unlimited amount, but can only take currency of a present value of 80,000 ptas out of the country, unless the transfer is made through a convertible account in a Spanish or Canary bank. You can write euro-cheques, which are cashed everywhere, for a maximum of 25,000 ptas (see GTT: Banks and Exchange Offices).

Getting there

Most travellers reach the Canary Islands by charter flight. It takes between four and six hours to fly there from the centre of Europe. Along with scheduled flights which fly direct from most large European cities to the two main islands Tenerife and Gran Canaria, there are also boats which go to the archipelago from Genoa or Cádiz. There are many flights and boats between the islands (see BII: Air Connections and Boat Connections). The Compañia Trasmediterránea runs a route between Cádiz – Tenerife – Gran Canaria – Lanzarote – Cádiz. The crossing from Cádiz to Tenerife takes 41 hours, to Gran Canaria 47.5 hours (including a harbour stop), to Lanzarote 60 hours. There is a summer and winter timetable. Meliá travel agents are the general agent. Trasmediterránea also runs the ferry routes between the islands. There is an agency in every island capital.

Gofio

A roasted meal of corn, wheat or barley handed down from the original Canary people. Dough cakes can be made from it or a dough can be formed in the zurrón, a goats leather pouch, by adding a little water. The natives use gofio to bind soups together, it goes well with muesli and, when stirred into a milky coffee, it makes a nutritious breakfast.

Guanches

The original inhabitants of the archipelago which were virtually wiped out by Spanish conquerors. The name is mistakenly used for all the original Canary inhabitants, although it is only really accurate for Tenerife; *guan* means son of Tenerife.

Language

It is useful to have some knowledge of the language especially on the smaller islands. In the tourist centres more and more people are learning English and other European languages. Of course, it is best to take a dictionary along. Here, below, is a little initial help. You are also refered to the chapter **Dictionary of Food and Drink**, which is preceded by some tips on pronunciation.

Words and Phrases

Good moring/Good day	Buenos días
Good afternoon	Buenas tardes
Good evening/Good night	Buenas noches
Goodbye	Hasta la vista/Adios
See you later	Hasta luego
Please	por favor
Thankyou	(muchas) gracias
yes/no	si/no
Mr/Mrs/Miss	señor/señora/señorita
Excuse me	Perdone
Do you speak English?	¿Habla Usted inglés?
Where is …?	¿Donde está …?
the street/the hotel	la calle/el hotel
right/left	derecha/isquierda
above/below	arriba/abajo
Is there a … here?	¿Hay por aqui …?
toilet	lavabó
room	habitación
room with a bathroom	habitación con baño
full board	con pension completa
everything included	todo incluido
How much is …?	¿Cuánto cuesta …?
bill	la cuenta
help	socorro
Where is a doctor/chemist?	¿Dónde hay un médico/una farmacia?
I need medecine for …	Necesito un medicamento contra …
How are you?	¿Como esta usted? (formal, aquaintance) ¿Que tal? (friendly)
good	bien
My name is …	Me llamo …
flight departure	salida
flight arrival	llegada
What time is it?	¿Qué hora es?
yesterday/today/tomorrow	ayer/hoy/manana
How far …?	¿Qué distancia …?

Numbers

0 cero	41 cuarenta y uno
1 uno (un) (una)	50 cincuenta
2 dos	51 cincuenta y uno
3 tres	60 sesenta
4 cuatro	61 sesenta y uno
5 cinco	70 setenta
6 seis	71 setenta y uno
7 siete	80 ochenta
8 ocho	81 ochenta y uno
9 nueve	90 noventa
10 diez	91 noventa y uno
11 once	100 ciento (cien)
12 doce	101 ciento uno
13 trece	110 ciento diez
14 catorce	127 ciento veintisiete
15 quince	200 doscientos/as
16 dieciseis	300 trescientos/as
17 diecisiete	400 cuatrocientos/as
18 dieciocho	500 quinientos/as
19 diecinueve	600 seiscientos/as
20 veinte	700 setecientos/as
21 veintiuno	800 ochocientos/as
30 treinta	900 novecientos/as
31 treinta y uno	1000 mil
40 cuarenta	1 Mio un millon

Days

Monday: *lunes*
Tuesday: *martes*
Wednesday: *miércoles*
Thursday: *jueves*
Friday: *viernes*
Saturday: *sábado*
Sunday: *domingo*

Months

January: *enero*
February: *febrero*
March: *marzo*
April: *abril*
May: *mayo*
June: *junio*
July: *julio*
August: *agosto*
September: *septiembre*
October: *octubre*
November: *noviembre*
December: *diciembre*

Long Distance Calls

(see GTT: Phoning)

Lucha canaria

(see GTT: Sport)

Maps and Plans

There are special island maps and town or tourist centre maps on all the islands. The *Mapa Turistico* on a scale of 1:150,000 is especially wide spread. It includes maps of the seven main Canary islands and a map of the towns of Las Palmas de Gran Canaria and Santa Cruz de Tenerife. The AA and RAC usually also have maps of the archipelago.

Medical Insurance

Spain has an agreement with some other European countries that you can be treated without having to pay the full cost, in case of illness. However, the procedure at the Spanish social services is slightly different from elsewhere. You will need an authorisation that you can get either from the DHSS or your private health scheme before you leave. If you fall ill, you simply need to hand this authorisation in to one of the branches of the Instituto Nacional de Prevision:

on Gran Canaria:
Avda. Juan XXIII, 2
Las Palmas
on Fuerteventura:
Avda. General Franco
Puerto Rosario
on Lanzarote:
Calle Fajardo, 2
Arrecife

on Tenerife:
Calle General Gutiérrez
Santa Cruz
on La Palma:
Calle Real, 22
Santa Cruz
on El Hierro:
in the Delegación del Gobierno building
Valverde
on La Gomera:
Calle Ruiz Padron, 22
San Sebastían

Music

The Canary people like to sing and play music. It is often the case that someone will spontaneously pick up the guitar or *timple*, the string instrument which originates from Lanzarote and which is similar to the ukelele. *Seguidillas* are the most popular songs, the texts of which are usually just made up as they go along. *Folias* are also popular – they are rhythmical, passionately played songs about everyday life, about love and work, food and drink. They are thought to come from Portugal.

Newspapers

Newspapers and magazines arrive on the islands two to three days after they are published (sometimes more). They are considerably more expensive. There are regional newspapers in English (and German and Norwegian), but these are mostly of poor quality, uncritical and are more like advertising papers.

Nudist Beaches

Nudist bathing is tolerated on some of the more remote beaches.

Phoning

It is cheapest to make calls either from the post office or from a public telephone box (it costs twice as much in hotels). A public telephone takes 5 ptas coins (for local calls), and 25 and 100 ptas coins. You will need to insert at least three coins at the start. Most telephone boxes have detailed information. First you should dial 07 (for abroad). Once there is a higher dialing tone, dial the prefix for your country.

Great Britain	44
Ireland	353
Germany	49
Denmark	45
Norway	47
Sweden	46
Finland	358
Austria	43
Switzerland	41

Now dial the code for the desired town (without the 0) and the telephone number.

Photography

Because of the unusually bright light, it is better not to take a fast (highly sensitive) film (lower DIN number).

Photosafari

Some tour operators offer day trips in jeeps. You travel away from the well known routes and can take the opportunity to look for other subjects.

Political Structure

The Canary Islands are part of Spain. The individual regions have formed autonomous governments which are under the control of the central government in Madrid. The government on the Canary Islands is the autonomous government of the Canary Region. The Spanish Home Office is represented in Las Palmas de Gran Canaria and in Santa Cruz de Tenerife by the *Gobierno Civil*. There are also branches of the Madrid ministries. Every island has its own administrative authority, the *Cabildo Insular*.

Population

1,445,000 inhabitants live on the 7,273 square metres which makes up the entire area of the archipelago. Las Palmas de Gran Canaria alone has 367,000 inhabitants, Santa Cruz de Tenerife, 191,000 – they are the two most important cities. The Canary people are a mixed race of original Canary people (*guanches*) and Spaniards. There are also Norman, Flemish and ' Arab influences. There is a slight difference between the people on each island, but on the whole there are no great differences. In general the Canary people are kind and hospitable, but keep some distance. They are proud, appreciate good behaviour, conservative and most of them are catholic. The official language is Castillian, but dialect is spoken on the streets. It has Latin-american traits and varies from island to island.

Prices

Since prices are constantly on the increase it makes little sense to give details. In the tourist centres things usually cost about as much as in Europe, but some of the supermarkets have rather inflated prices. In the centre of the islands you can still live quite cheaply. Here are some guidelines:

- Double room from 2,500 ptas upwards
- Apartments, depending on the number of beds, between 5,000 and 10,000 ptas
- Breakfast between 250 and 800 ptas
- Set meal in a medium good restaurant 1,000 ptas
- Bottle of good wine at least 800 ptas. Local wine, served by the carafe, is cheaper in restaurants.
- 0.2 litre beer, *caña*, 100–175 ptas
- coffee between 60 and 150 ptas according to type and place.

Propane and Calor Gas

You can get gas from supermarkets and petrol stations by exchanging your empty bottles. Non returnable and refillable bottles can be bought there too.

Provinces

The Canary region consists of two of the 52 Spanish provinces, the province of Santa Cruz de Tenerife encompassing the islands of La Palma, La Gomera and El Hierro and the province of Las Palmas de Gran Canaria, encompassing the islands of Gran Canaria, Fuerteventura and Lanzarote.

Public Holidays

Maundy Thursday (*Jueves Santo*), Good Friday (*Viernes Santo*) and Corpus Christi (*Corpus Christi*) are all on different dates each year. For the village festivals (*fiestas*), please see BII: Fiestas.

1 January
New Year's Day (*Año Nuevo*)
6 January
Feast of Epiphany (*Los Reyes*)
2 February
Candlemas (*La Candelaria*)
19 March
St. Joseph's Day (*San José*)
1 May
Mayday (*Día de Trabajo*)
29 June
Peter and Paul (*Pedro y Paulo*)
25 July
St. John's Day (*Santiago Apóstol*)
15 August
Assumption (*Asunción*)
12 October
Discovery of America (*Día de la Hispanidad*)
1 November
All Saints Day (*Todos los Santos*)
8 December
Immaculate Conception (*Immaculada Concepción*)
24 December
Christmas Eve (*La Nochebuena*)
25 December
Christmas Day (*Navidad*)

Settling in

Acclimatisation between two to three days. You should not expose yourself much to sun and sea in these days. Changing from a cool temperate, European climate to a subtropical one is often more difficult than one thinks.

Shopping

Since 1852 the Canary Islands have been a free trade zone, Tobacco, spirits and perfume are considerably cheaper than in Europe. Not every trader passes on the tax concessions to the customer, especially in the case of photographic or electrical goods. These goods should be tested very thoroughly. Bargaining is usual in Indian and Moroccan bazaars.

Souvenirs

Handfinished embroidery, called *calados*, which are made into the form of table cloths, sets, rugs and blouses, are among the more authentic souvenirs (beware of imitations). Patterned embroidery, *bordados*, come from La Palma along with black ceramics and basketware. Good quality ceramics can be found on all the islands. The Canary knives, which Canary farmers carry when working on the fields, are just as authentic. The knives are used at lunch or snack times and have decorative handles. On Lanzarote you can buy a *timple*, or Francigi miniatures. Along with stationery such as maps, calendars, brochures and books, natural produce is also a popular souvenir. For instance there are the delicious wines from El Hierro and Lanzarote or the banana liquer, a Canary speciality, handfinished cigars and bunches of strelitzia. Since the Canary Islands are a duty free zone, luxury goods are much cheaper. You should test both the good and

the price, since the concession is often not passed onto the customer or the good is of poor quality.

Spanish Tourist Board

Spanish National Tourist Board
57 St. James St
London SW1A
Tel. 071 499 0901

Sport

The Canary Islands are paradise for those who like sport. Almost all the larger hotels and some apartment blocks have sports facilities. There are tennis courts, some flood-lit, squash courts, volleyball courts and bowling alleys. You can play table tennis, minigolf, darts, you can arch or shoot. It is also possible to ride in some places. There are golf courses on Lanzarote, Fuerteventura and Gran Canaria. You can learn to hang-glide or go-cart racing on Gran Canaria. You can also learn to fly, go hiking or mountain climbing. Naturally, water sports are the most popular:

Deep sea fishing You can take part in deep sea fishing expeditions from Lanzarote, Fuerteventura, Gran Canaria and Tenerife. Tuna fish, bonitos, barracudas, sharks, marlins and wahoos are hunted. The most sought-after trophy is the swordfish. Puerto Rico in the south of Gran Canaria is the centre of big-game fishing. There is a conurbation with a yacht and fishing harbour there.

Vela latina

Sailing   There are sailing schools, Törns and boat hire places on all the islands. The Canary waters are known as a rich hunting ground due to the trade winds.

Surfing   The south of Fuerteventura and the south and south west coast of Gran Canaria are surfers' paradises The wind is very strong. There are surf schools on nearly all the islands, where you can also borrow boards.

Diving   There are many diving bases on Gran Canaria and Tenerife, which are run by diving schools. You can learn to dive on all the islands. If you prefer to go diving off your own back, you should get information on the currents before you go. Underwater hunting is not allowed along all the coast lines and it is completely forbidden with a tank and pneumatic harpoon. You may only hunt using a snorkel and elastic harpoon. You should look out for the jelly fish (*Physallia carabella*), which comes ashore in the early part of the year. If its 6–7 cm long tentacles touch you they can deliver a nasty sting which can bring on signs of paralysis. You will encounter some of the sea creatures which are mentioned in the capital **Fishing**. You should try and avoid the moray whose blood and bite are poisonous. There are no dangerous sharks which come near the shore. It is exciting to watch the nailray, which swims like a bird flies; its span can be as much as 2.5 m. It buries itself in the sand, where it can be recognised by the outline it leaves on the earth.

Waterskiing   Waterskiing and parachute gliding are on offer at the larger holiday resorts.

The Canary people adore football and basketball; bullfighting is not so popular, but is shown on Gran Canaria and Tenerife. On La Palma a sort of pole vaulting, *salto del regaton*, has survived. *Lucha canaria*, Canary wrestling is widespread on all the islands except Gomera.

Lucha canaria   *Lucha canaria* is a little reminiscent of Celtic wrestling, but it is thought to exist in this form only on the Canary Islands. According to other sources, it was also practiced in Egypt. Parallels can be seen in the reliefs at Beni Hassan, where two-men fights are depicted, which may substantiate this claim. It is a typical sport of the original Canary people, who liked to measure their strength at their village festivals. It is the same today. *Lucha canaria* is on the agenda of every village festival and the fighting place, the *terrero*, is prepared. The *terrero* is a double ring with stamped down earth or wood shavings. The inner ring measures 10 m, the outer 11 m. The wrestlers are called *pollos* (fighting roosters) and, as long as they are successful, are feted like football stars here. They wear a thin shirt and short linen trousers, which are rolled up at the bottom. It is here that the opponent holds on. The *pollos* fight bare foot. The fight is fair and this is shown by the ritual of entry. One team has 11 wrestlers. A maximum of three rounds, each round lasting up to 3 minutes, are fought. The wrestler who can throw his opponent three times, wins. This must take place within the inner ring or between the inner and outer ring on condition that the winner remains in the inner ring. The winner can fight a maximum of another three times. Every wrestler has to fight every member of the other team. The best of them know how to do all of the 43 grips which are allowed. Beginners must have mastered at least five of them.

Cockfighting is pursued mainly on Las Palmas de Gran Canaria and La Palma between February and May.

Cane Fighting (Fencing) Cane fighting is also of ancient origin. Earlier, the canefighter's aim was simply to defend himself against attackers, without having to kill or seriously injure him. The sport is divided into two variations: fencing with pliable rods, called *varas*, and fencing with *palos*, rough sticks. The players are not allowed to move their feet from the spot, so they can only parry the thrusts or move their upper body out of the way. When the sport is played with sticks, the aim is to move the body as little as possible. Only men play using a rod; when the sport is played with a stick there are also contests between men and women.

Time

Time in the Canaries is the same as GMT in winter; from the last Sunday in March to the last Sunday in September it is one hour ahead.

Time for Travelling

The Canary Islands' mild climate means that one can visit the whole year round. The temperature of the water is between 18°C in winter and 22°C in summer. There are cold and rainy days in winter and in summer, particularly on the eastern islands and in the south of Tenerife and Gran Canaria, it can be unbearably hot when the Sirocco is blowing and the desert wind heats the air up to 50°C and loads it with sand. Plants and flowers are in bloom from December to May and the vegetation is at its most sumptuous. The most pleasant time of year is from May to July/ August.

Tips

One generally leaves between 5 and 10%. A 15% service charge is included in hotel and restaurant bills. One should tip chamber maids at least 500 ptas per week. Otherwise tips are normally given to waiters, barkeepers, taxidrivers, tour guides, excursion bus drivers, ushers, porters and doormen.

Traffic Regulations

(see GTT: Driving)

Valuable Objects

Take care of valuable items if you want to keep them. There are many thefts. You are advised not to leave anything in the car. In some hotels there are safes in the rooms. As a rule, valuable objects can be given in to reception for security.

FOR YOUR NOTE

FOR YOUR NOTE

FOR YOUR NOTE

Index

182